THE COMPLET...

PRESERVING YOUR OWN SEEDS FOR YOUR GARDEN

Everything You Need to Know Explained Simply

KATIE A. MURPHY

The Complete Guide to Preserving Your Own Seeds for Your Garden: Everything You Need to Know Explained Simply

Copyright © 2011 by Atlantic Publishing Group, Inc.
1405 SW 6th Ave. • Ocala, Florida 34471 • 352-622-1825 • 352-622-1875–Fax
Website: www.atlantic-pub.com • E-mail: sales@atlantic-pub.com
SAN Number: 268-1250

Library of Congress Cataloging-in-Publication Data

Murphy, Katie A., 1979-
 The complete guide to preserving your own seeds for your garden : everything you need to know explained simply / by: Katie A. Murphy.
     p. cm.
Includes bibliographical references and index.
ISBN-13: 978-1-60138-352-5 (alk. paper)
ISBN-10: 1-60138-352-5 (alk. paper)
1. Seeds--Collection and preservation. 2. Gardening. I. Title.
SB118.38.M87 2011
631.5'21--dc22

                        2011012518

Printed in the United States

Over the years, we have adopted a number of dogs from rescues and shelters. First there was Bear and after he passed, Ginger and Scout. Now, we have Kira, another rescue. They have brought immense joy and love not just into our lives, but into the lives of all who met them.

We want you to know a portion of the profits of this book will be donated in Bear, Ginger and Scout's memory to local animal shelters, parks, conservation organizations, and other individuals and nonprofit organizations in need of assistance.

– Douglas & Sherri Brown,
President & Vice-President of Atlantic Publishing

Author Dedication

There's no one I know who better understands the value of family and commitment than my brother, Sean. He taught me to love the therapy of gardening, but more than that, he has shown me what selflessness truly is. Thanks, Sean.

Table of Contents

Chapter 3: Getting the Seed you Need 41

Chapter 4: Where Do Seeds Come From? 49

Chapter 7: Harvesting Mature Seeds 81

Chapter 8: Vegetables 87

Chapter 9: Fruits 143

Chapter 10: Flowers and Ornamentals 187

Chapter 11: Getting Things Started 217

Chapter 12: Places, Please 229

Chapter 13: Some Things to Grow On 237

Conclusion: Get Out There and Save Seeds 251

Appendix A: Quick Reference Planting Guide........................... 255

INTRODUCTION:
Encouraging Words for the Home Gardener

I grew up in the hot, humid sunshine of south Florida in a small, suburban home on less than one-fourth acre in the same house as my mother, brothers, sister, and grandparents. We had a little front yard and a little backyard, little extra money, and little extra time. Somehow, we always had flowers, fruit, and little garden vegetables growing despite all of our limitations.

Mom had her favorites, among them gardenias and sunflowers. Our front yard was always fragrant from the gardenia bushes and often dressed with tall, bright yellow sunflowers, both of which would grow almost year-round, with no harsh winter to impede on them. There was very little lawn, as lawns are difficult to grow in the sandy soil of Miami, which was ripe with ants and overwhelmed by crabgrass, so my family just grew plants — lots of plants.

All along the chain-link fence that separated the yard from the sidewalk were my grandmother's prized yellow roses, some dozen or so rose bushes that formed a protective hedge and blessed our yard with a little bit of beauty in an otherwise concrete jungle. My grandmother planted these roses when her only son left to join the Marine Corps. They served as a reminder to the family of his sacrifice on behalf of others.

The neighborhood otherwise was a wasteland of crime, graffiti, and unsightly litter, but our yard was a haven with birds of paradise, yellow roses, bright white gardenias, a few palms, exotic orchids, an umbrella tree, a sea grape tree, a large pine tree, some hedges, and whatever we gathered from friends and neighbors. My personal favorite was lantana, which grew as a weed along the city sidewalks. I would gather the flowers and bury them in the front yard, hoping they would grow. That was, of course, before I ever learned anything about how plants actually reproduce.

Our backyard consisted of a chicken coop with about a dozen chickens, whose eggs we sold to neighbors and whose manure we harvested for our gardens. There were also a few sheds with a woodworking shop where my grandfather built a structure my grandmother used to raise her prized orchids. It was her own little garden greenhouse, except in that part of Florida, it is never really cool enough to need an enclosed greenhouse, so it was mostly trellising. In it, my grandmother spent many hours tending to her beautiful flowering orchids, as well as doing any potting, sowing, or other garden tasks she desired. (Sometimes, I think she would just hide out there to have a little peace and quiet, away from the chaotic house.)

Her workroom was nestled in the far corner of the backyard, right between a decades-old avocado tree that was ornamented with hanging stag horns the size of small cars and a hedge of bougainvillea, which protected the property from intruders with its spiky thorns. The tree produced avocados that were usually about the size of a gallon-sized milk jug. We often had avocados from the backyard with dinner. One of our childhood chores was to scour for freshly fallen fruit that we would place in brown paper bags to ripen for dinners. Once we ate the fruit, grandma would take the large seed, skewer it with three toothpicks like a tripod, and set it halfway in a cup of water in the windowsill to begin a new tree. She planted some of these trees, but gave many more away to neighbors and friends. In this way, the avocado was my first experience with harvesting seeds for growth.

In addition to these other plants, my family also had a mango tree that grew on the property line in the corner of the other three yards we neighbored. The fruit that fell in our yard was ours to keep. We also grew limes, grapefruit, and oranges from time to time, though due to citrus canker threat, these trees were eventually eradicated in our area. But for a time, we often feasted on fruit salad for dinner.

When we bought pineapples at the grocery store, my grandmother saved the tops and planted them in our side yard. These grew into new pineapple plants that were just as tasty as the ones that came from Hawaii. We also would collect and trade the sea grapes to neighborhood kids for their nectarines and oranges.

I was often fortunate enough to be able to take trips up the coast to visit my aunt in Merritt Island, Florida. She kept some of the sweetest grapefruit known to the state (at least in my opinion), and her gardens were tropical and lush, fragrant, and colorful. It was in her front yard that I discovered plumeria, a sweet, nectar flower nearly as fragrant as gardenia and every bit as lovely.

We also lived very close to my great-grandmother's horse ranch. She had a lime tree in her side yard with a stag horn so big it bent the tree over and down to the ground. This lime tree was at least 25 years old and still produced amazing fruit. Great-grandma also had a vegetable garden where she grew lots of tomatoes. She and my great-grandfather owned a restaurant and were chefs; they prized their vegetable garden almost as much as their own home.

My older brother had the opportunity to go to a vocational high school that focused on horticulture. He learned many practices and brought them home to implement in our yard. I observed as he grafted orange trees, pruned roses into perfectly shaped bushes, grew herbs and flowers we never had before, and brought my grandmother's struggling elephant ear plant to vibrancy. He had a truly green thumb and made me realize that gardening was not just an interesting hobby that belonged to past generations; it was in our blood.

As I was coming into my own, I was fortunate enough to live for a while on a south Miami property that was a couple acres large. It was a beautiful log cabin on a densely wooded lot. The property's owners loved many of the same plants I grew up with, like stag horns, but they also had several fruit trees in an orchard in the backyard surrounding the pool. Much like our avocados and mangoes, their family often delighted in fresh grapefruit, oranges, lemons, and Key limes that grew on the thorniest trees I had ever known to that day. True Key lime pie is very different than just lime pie, and with fresh Key limes from the backyard, it is remarkably good.

I left that temporary home for the Air Force, which took me all over the United States. I experienced plants I had never seen before that could not grow in the South Florida heat. My newfound love of horticulture was met with an endless supply of new experiences. I learned lantana was not just a sidewalk weed. I discovered hydrangea in Virginia, and completely lined my home with them, experimenting with acidity and alkalinity of their soil (which changes the color of the flowers). I found all of my new favorites — crepe myrtle trees, azalea, maple, rudbeckia, columbine, and more — across the vast landscape of the country.

In Virginia, I became an accidental master gardener, taking classes at community centers, winning awards for my small home garden, and volunteering hundreds of hours at community gardens. The title was inadvertent; I earned it in passing while doing something I truly enjoyed. My passion for horticulture was alive and well. My garden filled with hostas, pansies, snapdragons, dianthus, azaleas, hydrangeas, gardenias (which were not known to grow so far north), roses, hollyhock. Many more varieties earned me daily visits from neighbors, and we began trading seeds.

Gardening became a neighborhood practice, improving the lives of my own family and those who shared in the hobby. We grew a small community vegetable garden (this was all in base housing on Langley Air Force Base) with rows of beans, peas, wintergreens, herbs, carrots, potatoes, tomatoes, and peppers. Saving seeds from these plants and using them to grow many generations, we all supplemented lunches and dinners with our crops and enjoyed a strong sense of community from our garden.

While I was away, my family sold my childhood home and moved to northern Florida. They still have no lawns, as the soil is still as sandy and problematic, but on the several acres mom and grandma own, there are bountiful plants. All the wonderful things they could not grow further south now grow in abundance. My brother still tends to my mom's gardens and his own, and my grandmother and grandfather now have a small farm and orchard, as well as a beautiful landscape. There are still gardenias and yellow roses aplenty, and now hollyhock and hydrangea thrive as well. In fact, the hollyhock sprouting in my garden in Oklahoma is from the seeds of my grandmother's plant in Florida, which were the children of mine that grew in Virginia, and siblings to those of various friends and neighbors in Colorado and Texas.

Now, as I settle into my new home in Oklahoma, I have just enough room for a small flower garden with my few favorite plants to keep my home inviting. I will undoubtedly spend my extra hours doing community gardening and growing things indoors with my own children to ignite the spark in them. Gardening is more than just a hobby; it is a lifestyle. It is a bond that connects generations and builds communities. It is a manifestation of natural desires to be productive and master the environment. It is therapeutic, and it is valuable.

Whether you have acres, or a few feet in front of a condominium; whether you are in the far extremes of the South or at the highest altitudes; or whether you have a lofty budget, many resources, and lots of time, or very little of the three, gardening is an accessible, worthwhile endeavor. Gardening has many tangible benefits, including enhancing the beauty of the environment around you, increasing air quality, and growing healthy foods.

This book seeks to help you become the gardener you desire to be. It will help the home gardener perpetuate the plants you already possess and those that you will plant and grow in the future. It will help you find ways to not just grow your plants, but grow your garden, widen its horizons, and mold it to produce what you require of it. It will not tell you what you want to grow — that part is up to you — but it will make recommendations for plants that are easier to grow and propagate (reproduce) from seed.

I will cover the reproductive life of plants and how they procreate, using that information to assist the natural reproductive process to meet your needs as a gardener. I also will cover hundreds of specific plants and how to harvest life from them in the form of seeds. It is my hope that this book will be a detailed resource for you, the home gardener, with well-worn, weathered pages that inspire rows of bountiful crops and lush beds of ornamentals. I also wish you the absolute joy that gardening has brought me and my family over the years. Happy harvesting!

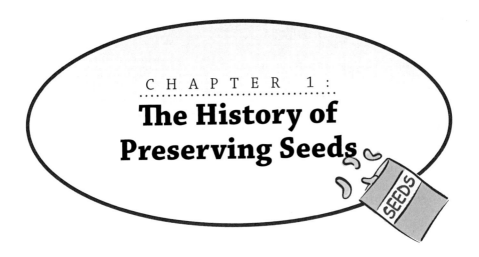

C H A P T E R   1 :
The History of Preserving Seeds

Gardening long served an important role in society. From earliest history, primitive peoples relied on the food they harvested in addition to the spoils of a hunt for sustenance. As the human species developed in ability — using tools, communicating, and learning — sophistication in the garden also developed. No one knows exactly where and when man first deliberately gathered seeds for future use in the garden, but the evidence of this learned behavior dates back to very early civilizations.

Origins of Seed Preservation

Many historians believe that wheat was the first grain man cultivated, with evidence of its planting dating back more than 10,000 years in the Middle East. The citizens of Jericho sowed two varieties of wheat (emmer and einkorn), as well as barley around 8,000 B.C. As the first-known town with more than 2,000 residents, archaeologists attribute Jericho's successes to the ability to cultivate the land and produce a crop. A pioneering civilization on many accounts, with the ability to grow and harvest their own food, the citizens of Jericho advanced beyond their hunter-gatherer neighboring villages, requiring the city to build fortifications to protect its many assets, including propagated food.

In what is modern-day Mexico (the Tehuacán Valley), people first cultivated chili and squash as crops as long as 7,000 years ago. Corn (maize), beans, and gourds followed suit soon after. All these plants preceded rice as a crop, which did not occur until about 2,500 B.C., in either India or China.

Many more pieces of archaeological evidence show the most common plants still grown today have been used for thousands of years. There have been as many generations of plants as there are years between those early cultivars and the ones that exist now. Some cultivars carry large genetic differences due to environmental changes, migrations, people intentionally growing plants with characteristics they desire, and so on. Regardless, people still use many plants like just like their ancestors did. From the beginning, **horticulturists** — those who practice cultivating plants in a garden or nursery — from around the world recognized and cherished the legacy of seeds and the numerous gifts they give us. They are food but also serve to provide clothing (cotton, hemp), medicine and holistic therapy (Echinacea, tea), shelter (straw as thatched roofing, timber), and tools (plant fibers as twine, gourds as ladles, spoons, and bowls). They are a source of natural beauty, refreshing and fragrant, and improve the air surrounding us. Their value lies in both form and function.

Because of their inherent importance, the earliest gardeners saved and preserved the seeds from the plants they used, sowing their seeds across the landscape as they migrated to new frontiers. They collected new varieties and improved their crops. Sometimes they thrived (as in Jericho) and sometimes they failed (as did Americans in the Dust Bowl), but they gained a better understanding of the natural environment and amassed a collection of best practices in cultivation still passed on today.

Historians hold accounts throughout humankind's historical narrative of seed saving. Cultivated crops emerged as the main source of food for man and his animals and were often so valuable that civilizations periodically bartered seeds. Mayan and Aztecan societies even used seeds such as cacao and chia as currency, with cacao actually considered sacred.

Europeans traveled to the farthest corners of the unexplored world and returned home with precious seeds from the new lands they had visited. In fact, explorers discovered and settled the Americas while racing to find a more efficient trade route for spices grown in places like India and China. Leaders of European nations spent vast resources on developing trade routes because many of the seeds that were so highly developed could not be grown in Europe. Europeans still enjoy many plants from explorers' yields by cultivating the seeds successfully brought back on their own soil. Thus, plants and seeds played a significant role in finding and developing the New World.

When establishing settlements in the Americas, Europeans arrived with carefully guarded seeds from home, hoping the seeds would thrive and become their initial supply of food while exploring their new environment. Fortune held for many settlers, and they successfully colonized the Americas. In turn, some of them traveled back to the European continent with indigenous seeds like corn, which at the time was unknown to Europeans.

Among his other missions, Captain James Cook explored the Pacific Islands in part to bring back specimens and seeds of the breadfruit plant. Sailors demanded breadfruit because it was easy to cultivate and harvest aboard ship, and they used it for food during their long ocean voyages. Sir Walter Raleigh brought plants and seeds back to England as well, introducing the Europeans to the wildly popular and addictive nicotiana (tobacco) plant.

Seeds do not just carry historical significance in the migration of societies and exploration and conquering of new lands. Seeds also carry a great deal of importance in the fabric of society. The story of Jack and the Beanstalk is more than just a parable with a warning against imprudent decisions. It demonstrates the value of the tiny seed with exponential potential. The Biblical tale of the faith of a mustard seed is another instance of such great value assigned to such a small biological wonder. The seed is a symbol of potential and promise, of fertility and regeneration. *The Good Earth* by Pearl S. Buck follows a Chinese rice farming family through feast and famine, and *The Grapes of Wrath* by John Steinbeck is about an Oklahoma farm family forced off their land in the 1930s because they lost their ability to cultivate seed into crop.

Seed Preservation Today

American pioneers are responsible for planting seeds, which to this day represent crops still cultivated across the United States and Canada. Today, those gardening practices that happened throughout history still endure and prevail in every agricultural society on earth. Scientists at the University of Wisconsin-Madison estimated total organic and nonorganic farming (including pasture used for grazing for livestock) consumed approximately 40 percent of the Earth's arable land in 2005, compared to about 7 percent in 1700.

Heirloom tomatoes

In the last quarter century, seed saving and preservation reemerged as a cherished gardening practice. Heirloom fruit, flowers, and vegetables are back in force in their rightful place — the home garden. **Heirloom plants** are plant species handed down through generations, like a prized wedding ring or an ages-old family portrait. Many families keep these traditions and pass on seeds, with grandchildren enjoying the same heirloom fruits, flowers, and vegetables that their grandparents did. There is no genetic engineering, complex scientific alteration, or hormones. What sits on the plate or in the vase is an unaltered grandchild of the plant from great-grandmother's garden.

While some people preserve plants for their personal enjoyment, there are other reasons people opt to preserve seeds and grow their own plant varieties. One such reason is the assurance of the means by which the plants are grown — the use or non-use of chemical fertilizers, pesticides, hormones, or herbicides. The increasing desire for organically grown foods is evidence that consumers are aware of the harmful effects chemical pesticides have on those who consume traditionally grown produce and foods. People reverted to home gardening to satisfy their desires for quality-grown food that carries no unnecessary carcinogenic risk for them and are interested in preserving seeds to make such home gardening more affordable and sustainable.

Some gardeners preserve seeds for hobby and some for health, while another group of people save seeds for survival. There are many reasons survival gardeners save and preserve seeds. While some believe in the impending doom facing civilization, be it Armageddon or some other end-time prophecy, others simply believe there is a likelihood of natural disaster on a large scale that will impact life as we know it, to the extent that having a stash of seeds ready to grow will ultimately lead to the survival of their families. Some seed companies cater to the needs of these individuals and even sell ready to use seed vaults that contain all the preserved seeds a person needs to survive through a "the end of the world as we know it" situation. Typical seed vaults are actually not vaults at all, but rather airtight containers housing a few pounds of various types of seeds, usually 25 to 30 varieties with about 50,000 seeds. A 1.5-pound seed vault, containing 50,000 nonhybrid seeds of 25 plant varieties, is available from Heirloom Organics (www.non-hybrid-seeds.com/sp/survival-seed-vault.html) and another, containing 35 plant varieties in 22,000 seeds, is sold by Hometown Seeds (**www. hometownseeds.com/survival-seeds-c-213/survival-seeds-peace-of-mind-for-your-family-p-35**).

In addition to these considerations, many economists and agriculturists around the world believe that with the increasing demand for produce and the ever-shrinking availability of farmland to expand into, prices for produce will grow higher and higher. Accordingly, they believe this trend will continue until the market eventually cannot fill the need, and a food shortage will occur. People with their own food supplies will not have to face many of the hardships it is believed people depending on the economy to provide their food will — standing in bread lines, dealing with ration stamps and cards, and going without altogether. Of course, this is only one theory, but there is evidence already that it is an increasing likelihood. Those people who preserve and grow their own seeds, and have the knowledge to do so into the future, will be better equipped to endure this kind of hardship.

Around the globe, widespread legislation threatens to control seed preservation and distribution. In the recent past, Great Britain revised and loosened their seed legislation. Initially, gardeners could only use, trade, and sell from a list of acceptable seed varieties. The legislation was created to ensure that the integrity and genetic diversity of seeds was maintained, and the responsibility was on commercial growers to determine what varieties to invest their time and money into preserving. However, it also meant that certain heirloom varieties that did not have the perceived popularity or backing by commercial growers risked falling into obscurity.

Many other nations are restricting the free trade of seeds by farmers and gardeners in much the same way as Great Britain's original legislation, allowing only commercial companies to distribute seed. In some cases, commercial growers lobby ill-informed legislators, assuring them these restrictions are in the best interest of the nation's agricultural stability, but in reality, commercial growers can only sustain a small portion of the seed diversity that a network of small, independent growers can. Though intended to preserve the purity of seed stocks, these laws significantly restrict small farmers from conducting business as they often have for many generations. In India, the law dictates that farmers cannot even give away their surplus seed; it must be destroyed.

These types of laws are another major reason for the recent growth of individual interest in harvesting and saving seed. When governments begin to infringe on personal liberties, people take greater interest in preserving those liberties. In this case, people are actively taking measures to preserve their ability to provide food for themselves and their families and to run their businesses as they have grown accustomed to.

But seed legislation and government intervention is not all doom and gloom. In the United States, the National Center for Genetic Resources Preservation (NCGRP) maintains the largest of many thousands of seed banks around the world. With more than 475,000 accessions in its temperature and humidity-controlled Colorado facility, its mission is to ensure agriculture can survive in the event of global catastrophe or significant climate change. These accessions currently represent about half of the 10,000 species preserved nationally by the United States. NCGRP also maintains cooperation with the Svalbard Global Seed Vault, built in the arctic north to house and preserve a global collection of seeds. Other nations are attempting national seed preservation efforts as well, some successfully and others failing (as in Iraq where seed stockpiles were pillaged during war). Beginning with the first seed bank in Russia in 1894, the N.I. Vavilov All-Russian Scientific Research Institute of Plant Industry, and looking forward to future arctic preservation efforts, seed saving is a global effort.

The NCGRP collects its accessions mainly from small, independent growers across the country. Its collection is largely heirloom variety seeds. As an at-home gardener, like the smaller independent growers, you play an important role in preserving plant species when you harvest your own seed. Every generation a plant species succeeds ensures the line for posterity. In your backyard garden plot, you are making history, and as you pass your seeds on to friends and family, you are creating a legacy.

Benefits of Gardening and Saving Seeds

Gardening is widely regarded as one of the most therapeutic hobbies in which people engage. It is known to be calming and meditative, and it quenches a primal need to provide food to family and work the earth. It is an outlet for frustration and for creativity. It brings a measurable product in terms of quantity and quality, as well as intangibles like beauty. A plant rejuvenates a room more than a painting, purifies the air more than an air freshener, and is a one-of-a-kind living creature.

Of course, plants are food as well. Certain vitamins that are found in sufficient quantities solely in fruits and vegetables prevent disease and improve overall health. In third-world nations, certain nutritive diseases prevail. The World Health Organization of the United Nations (WHO) addresses many of these diseases on its website, **www.who.int**, including vitamin A deficiency (causing blindness), combatable by consuming simple garden vegetables like carrot, broccoli, and sweet potato. Scurvy, once common aboard ships, is easily staved off with vitamin C-rich foods. Consuming the plant foods that are routinely grown in the home garden fights beriberi, lesions, pellagra, pernicious anemia, rickets, neurological disease, hemorrhaging, and a variety of other conditions and diseases.

Economically speaking, gardening is a more cost-effective way to provide many of these dietary staples. Studies conducted by the National Gardening Association indicate that with an initial $70 investment in seed, tools, and fertilizer and about 600 square feet of garden space, the average annual vegetable garden yield is $530 in produce. A savvy gardener who starts with seeds instead of plants can save even more and possibly produce even more (with heirloom varieties that thrive in the local environment). Even if starting from seed this year is not a possibility, in following years, starting from harvested seed will prove to be very cost-effective, nearly free. And even if you do not have 600 square feet to plant in, the estimated annual yield for a well-maintained garden is about a half pound per square foot, so any amount of gardening can save you money.

There are countless health benefits to gardening in addition to providing nutrition at a reduced cost. Working the land — bending, stooping, pulling, digging, raking, carrying — all benefit physical health and fitness. Fresh air and sunshine, which is a major source of vitamin D, also contribute significantly to health and wellness. Better overall health and lower stress levels are consistent traits found among regular gardeners.

Gardening and seed saving both also play important roles in family and community. Neighborhood gardens offer up locations for friends to come together for their own benefit and for that of the entire community. They learn new techniques from each other and pass along plants, seedlings, and seeds to share.

Sharing seeds occurs in more than the community garden plot. Seed cooperatives and seed exchanges are growing in popularity as gardeners seek less commercialized varieties of garden favorites, like heirloom tomatoes and beans. This is yet another cost-effective gardening practice that further increases the benefit to the home gardener.

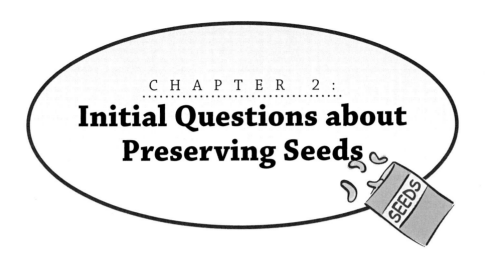

CHAPTER 2:

Initial Questions about Preserving Seeds

Where to Start

Most gardeners have a selection of favorite plants that they would like to continue to grow in their gardens. If this is your case, you will want to research the specific reproductive life of the plant you would like to harvest seed from to find out what its needs are, when and how it is fertilized, how it produces seed, and when the seed is ready for harvesting. This book will include many common and some lesser common garden plants and varieties with all the research complete for you. *If you do not have plants to harvest from, see Chapter 3, which describes in more detail readily available seed sources.* Once you have your seed and plant it, you will want to come back to this book to read about how to get it to produce viable seeds for the future.

Where Can You Grow Plants?

Is there any particular geographic region of the country that is more conducive to successful seed saving and preservation? The answer is no. If you are successful in growing plants in your area of the country, there should be nothing preventing you from saving and preserving the seeds from those plants, or any new plants that thrive from seeds you have acquired. Plants existed on the planet before humans or animals were present, and they thrive sometimes despite our best efforts to eradicate them (think of persistent weeds). Some plants are hardier than others and better able to survive, and conversely, some do not like human interference at all. Regardless their special needs, most plants take well to seed preservation and human assistance in propagation.

Rebirth of a forest that was destroyed by the eruption of Mount St. Helens

Plants are genetically predisposed for adaptation and survival. To understand the survival instinct that exists in the plant world, revisit the photographs from the aftermath of the volcanic eruption of Mount St. Helens that occurred in Washington in 1980. Remember the pictures of the seedlings sprouting through the volcanic ash? Those little evergreen seedlings grew with determination, even in the most drastically unfavorable conditions possibly imaginable.

Plants are like any other living, breathing organism. They want and need to live. Everything in their genetic makeup demands it. It is feasible to grow plants in nearly every location on earth, except where the cold temperature extremes make it impossible for plant life to survive.

That being said, you know which plants have given you the best results and were the easiest to grow with the least amount of effort. If you have limited experience in your own garden, visit a local botanical garden and ask questions, or seek the input of a neighbor with a thriving garden. Every environment possesses its own challenges, be it humidity, aridity, soil acidity or alkalinity, sun exposure, extreme cold, excessive heat, poor drainage, or even altitude. Knowing your environment and its problems will help you choose successful plants for your region. *Consult the quick reference section in Appendix 1 for ideas of plants that do well in your climate and region of the country, and start there.*

How Long Does it Take?

Depending on what you expect from your garden, it can be an easy, part-time hobby, or a time-consuming lifestyle. If you are looking for a few tomatoes and a couple green beans, you will have plenty of time for other things around your gardening. However, if you are considering a full-scale backyard garden, complete with cabbage, lettuce, carrots, potatoes, spinach, cucumbers, melons, strawberries, and all other types of delicious fresh treats, you can expect to spend considerably longer in the garden. In fact, if that is the scale you wish to achieve, you will likely be looking at a change in lifestyle if you are not already gardening.

This is not meant to discourage you in the least from gardening as much of your own food as possible. On the contrary, it is one of the healthiest choices you can make for yourself and your family, and one of the best returns on your time investment that you can make. Gardening is an economic decision to use less to get more. It is a decision to work and build strength and to eat more nutritiously. Its benefits are great, and its cost in time is disproportionately low.

While there are lulls in between growing seasons, in the diversified garden, during the warm weather months you will invariably have a garden task to complete. Whether it is removing weeds, watering, pruning, or other basics to maintain the health of the plants or to prepare a plant to pollinate and produce seeds, there are abundant tasks for the home gardener to perform. At the beginning of the growing season, expect to spend time preparing the soil, sowing seeds to start plants, and thinning the herd for the best samples to grow. Then you will be monitoring their growth, watching for blooms, deciding how many plants to breed and how many to eat, how to keep them from breeding on their own, and watching them develop seed for the next year's garden. You will harvest that seed and prepare it for its rest (and yours) before the next season starts anew. It is work, but it is also rewarding.

Look at all of the requirements of the plants you are planning to grow and harvest seed from. See what kind of attention they need and how routinely. You can take shortcuts on some things, like irrigation systems instead of hand watering, but assess fairly the amount of time each task takes and when. Include time to prepare soil and pots, sow seeds, transplant them, water, thin seedlings, emplace isolation techniques, pollinate, protect plants, move them, and gather and dry seeds. Stagger your plantings throughout the growing season to spread out your garden tasks, and then plan to be in the garden regularly. This way, you will never have too many tasks to complete at any one time.

How Much Room Do You Need?

A full vegetable, fruit, and flower garden for a single family over the course of a year can take up hundreds of square feet in the yard. To determine how much room you need, decide what you need from your garden. Again, a few plants can make a huge impact on a grocery bill and still take very little space. Some do not even require being planted or grown outdoors, let alone in mass quantities in the ground.

Growing a garden should be a gradual process for the inexperienced gardener. Start out with a few stable varieties that do well in your region and that you will enjoy (for example, do not grow peaches if you will not eat peaches). You should gradually increase your garden to fill both your available time and available space.

If you only have a patio at the back of your townhome or apartment, container gardening will be the only option for you, but you can do a lot with containers; strawberries and tomatoes do very well, for example. If you have many acres, you may have more space available, but time will still be a limiting factor for you. Can you successfully plant and harvest a full acre garden? Some certainly can, but others may find it overwhelming. Assess your needs and desires, look those plants up, see what their requirements are, and determine what you can fit in your garden.

For seed preservation, little room is needed besides the garden itself. You will want a work surface on which you may separate seeds from their pods, label and prepare them for storage, and adequate storage room (usually a dedicated shelf in the refrigerator for most kitchen gardens).

For some plants with special needs, you may need to find a dry, warm place to guard dug up plants or harvested seedpods while they dry. This can be a heated shed or garage, basement, or greenhouse. You may also need a root cellar or other arrangement to simulate damp, cool storage for plants over the winter. These requirements, though, depend on your region, climate, and your plants' specific needs.

Do You Need Special Equipment?

Example of a glass cloche

Though there are all types of specialized equipment you may purchase if you so desire, the majority of seed harvesting tasks require nothing more than a pair of garden scissors, a shovel, a good pair of gloves, and a bucket. Certainly, no expensive equipment is required. You can dry seeds on a tarp, a cookie sheet, or newsprint. You can collect silica gel packets from products you buy (shoes and luggage frequently have these packs inside) to keep in with your seeds to keep them dry while you store them. You can recycle clear jugs to use as cloches and insulate your plants. **Cloches** are small structures made of glass or clear plastic that are placed over cold-sensitive garden plants in cold weather (*Cloches are discussed in detail in Chapter 6.*). Window screening and two-by-fours make cages to isolate your plants. The salvage store can be your greatest friend in the garden, using old gates as trellises or old windows as a **cold frame** — a box with glass or clear plastic sides and an opening roof that also protects plants from cold. Community sharing and swapping sites like Craigslist (**www.craigslist.org**) and Freecycle (**www.freecycle.org**) often have salvage items posted by members that you can use in the garden as well. Anywhere this text describes a process requiring materials, it will recommend commonly available resources that cost little to nothing, or that most homes already have. The goal here is to make the process of saving seeds attainable for every home gardener.

CASE STUDY: PRESERVATION AND STORAGE TRICKS TO YIELD FRESH PRODUCT

Dan Jason
President, The Seed and Plant
Sanctuary for Canada; owner, Salt
Spring Seeds
Dan@saltspringseeds.com

Dan Jason is the president of the Seed and Plant Sanctuary for Canada and the owner of Salt Spring Seeds. Jason has been president of the sanctuary since 2002 and founded his mail-order seed business Salt Spring Seeds in 1986.

His passion for seed preservation began when he was a young teenager. "When I started to grow out unusual crops in the 80s, such as quinoa and amaranth, I realized the best way of popularizing them was to start my own seed company," Jason said. He is currently upholding his strong enthusiasm for saving seeds through the organizations he leads and the many books he has written.

Jason describes the process of saving seeds in four basic steps: selecting the seeds when they are ready, gathering the seeds, drying, and then storing them.

"Getting good seeds at the right time involves knowing the usual life cycle of a plant and whether a seed will stay true," Jason said. The means of gathering the seeds involves several different methods, such as plucking, rubbing, shaking, or grabbing.

Drying requires the preserver to have an appropriate drying space. This step helps prevent mold from accumulating. "Most seeds will dry adequately for home storage if spread on wax paper, newspapers, trays, plates, or screens in an airy place for a few days to a week," Jason said. He also said that letting the seed heads or stalks dry in open, paper bags for one or two weeks is an equally effective method.

When digging up plants for storage, Jason advises choosing healthy plants that show desirable characteristics to the variety. "Don't save seed from plants that bolt to seed the first season," Jason said.

To prepare roots for preservation, Jason dries and toughens the skin but leaves the root firm and plump through a process called curing. "Curing enables the root to resist molding and heals small breaks in the skin, which would otherwise invite decay," Jason said. He advises curing on a dry day when the soil is not too sodden.

Jason follows the three-step process below when curing:

1. Gently shake or rub off any excess earth.

2. At an inch above the crown, cut off the tops, and lay them to dry in the sun or indoors for about a day.

3. Turn them once to ensure that all areas are exposed to the air.

The fourth step of the basic series Jason describes for preservation is storage. This involves administering proper labels and containers for each type of seed. "It is wise to keep identifying sticks or markers with each variety at each step. When they are put away, they should get a label and date on their container," Jason said.

He also said that seeds should always be stored under cool, dry conditions. Sealing most seeds from air, except beans and peas, which need some air circulation, prolongs viability. He recommends placing the seeds in airtight tins, glass jars, or plastic containers and then setting them in the freezer.

Throughout Jason's experience, he has learned many tricks to preserve the natural and true genes of plants.

Jason recommends preserving self-pollinating annuals, such as lettuces, beans, grains, tomatoes, and peppers. "It is easy to save a diversity of them, and they are very significant crops to save," Jason said. Also, grains are one of the easiest crops to grow. On the contrary, there are few perennials that can be saved for seed, with the exception of chives, asparagus, and rhubarb.

Jason varies his growing techniques depending on each plant's method of pollination. For example, when growing cross-pollinating plants, he allows only one variety of each type of plant to flower. This eliminates the need for isolation.

He also said that barriers can be erected or planted, plantings can be staggered, or crops can be covered with fabric. If a plant, such as corn, is cross-pollinated by the wind, isolation is essential. When growing squash and pumpkins, Jason suggests fastening paper bags over the female flowers, dabbing pollen from the male flowers onto the females, and then closing the bag again to ensure genetic integrity.

As a general method to keep seed pure, Jason separates varieties by distance, barriers, time, or grows just one variety of crops. He also keeps seed from previous years in case an impurity develops among a crop.

Jason feels that saving seeds is especially important in today's society. "It is crucial that we keep growing out plant cultivars so that they can adapt to all the changes we are experiencing. We need many more people to preserve our heritage of seeds," Jason said.

Jason's experience has provided him a wealth of knowledge on the topic. His advice for beginning and experienced growers and preservers is to work with the crops that produce the best results for you and that you are most passionate about.

The Seed and Plant Sanctuary for Canada is becoming a living gene bank for edible and medicinal plants that can be grown in Canada. It is also a reference for growers and preservers who have questions about crops and saving seed. Lifetime membership in the sanctuary entitles you to five seed varieties in the collection every year as long as you inform the organization of the seed's progress. For more information, please visit The Seed and Plant Sanctuary for Canada at **http://seedsanctuary.com**.

Salt Spring Seeds provides untreated, open-pollinated, and non-GMO seeds to farmers and gardeners on their website. For more information, please visit Salt Spring Seeds at **http://saltspringseeds.com**.

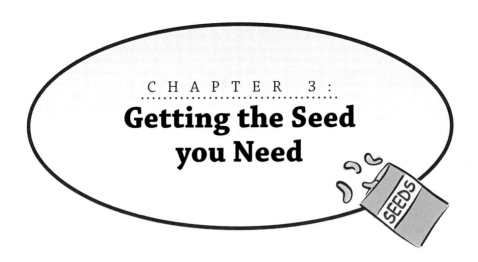

CHAPTER 3:

Getting the Seed you Need

Knowing where to find an initial supply of seeds is quintessential to starting the process of preserving seeds. A gardener who already has a garden may see this as a little easier to accomplish. Without a ready supply of harvest-worthy plants, there are a few other means of obtaining seeds. Garden centers and home improvement warehouses carry a wide variety of seeds that are ready for sowing. In addition, many gardeners engage in seed exchanges.

Some gardeners may also use less conventional means. For example, some have luck with dried beans from the grocery store in their gardens. Though quite unconventional, and certainly not guaranteed to work, bags of beans and peas — under the right circumstances — can also be used to grow plants. Though they might produce food, there is no way of knowing whether the beans or peas on the shelf will actually produce fertile seeds, as many types of these plants grown for food are hybrids and therefore, sterile.

Regardless of the means used to obtain the seed, the ultimate goal is perpetuating the plants desired in the garden through saving seeds and harvesting them in following years.

Buying the Pretty Envelopes

Why buy the plant when you can get the seed? The most cost-ineffective way to begin a garden from scratch is to purchase individual plants, which can range in price from 50 cents upward to $5 or $6 per plant. The home garden will require at least a few plants and probably in the hundreds, possibly thousands, depending on the size of the garden. Buying full-grown plants can cost thousands of dollars to populate a larger-scale home vegetable garden or a moderate landscaping endeavor.

Garden centers, home improvement warehouses, and even some big-box retailers stock a vast array of seeds (as well as bulbs, corms, and live plants) for the home gardener. This presents an attractive lure to any gardener — pretty envelopes, often with photographs of the most attractive specimen of that particular plant, and a lovely description of the product: "Fiery shades of red, orange, and burgundy," "Prized by gourmets as the most flavorful of all parsleys," or "Masses of petite, yellow, daisy-like flowers with chocolate brown button centers." Not only do the new flowers promise to be "irresistible to butterflies," but also they are practically irresistible to the shopper.

Before purchasing the pretty envelopes, the gardener should know some things about packaged seeds. Most garden centers stock seed that is best when planted in the near-term. The means that seed is in season or almost in season and usually less than a year from its harvest date. In this way, the gardener benefits from fresher, more viable seed without needing to wait countless months and worry about details of preservation before using the seed. However, it also limits the gardener who cannot effectively plan a plant rotation because the next season's selection of commercially available seed is widely unknown. A grower or nursery may choose an entirely different type of tomato to produce seed for next year that the gardener may not prefer.

The packaged seeds often eliminate the unknown, which may be one of their greatest benefits to a lesser-experienced gardener. The packaging tells where to plant, in what type of soil, at what temperature, with how much light and water, and any other care needed. It also often details how to thin out the plants effectively for optimal growth, tips for starting early and transplanting, and other useful information. Generally, seeds commercial growers sell have to meet a certain minimum viability (ratio of seeds that will grow to overall seeds).

All of that comes at a premium, as well. Seed packets cost on average $1 to $3. A single package or two is not a huge investment, but starting an entire garden from seed packets can prove very expensive. Think of a vegetable garden containing two varieties of tomatoes, carrots, a few varieties of leafy greens, several common herbs, celery, and so on. What seems like an inexpensive undertaking can add up quickly. Several hundred dollars can produce an extensive vegetable garden, which is less expensive than landscaping plants, but still quite expensive.

The cost of seed compared to the cost of starter plants is more appealing. Once the initial investment is made, the gardener can enjoy years of fruits, vegetables, and flowers at a fraction of the cost compared to starting with plants. Deciding whether to use seeds or starter plants (or possibly which combination of plants and seed) will depend on budget, but also on the time available to the gardener to start plants from scratch. Seeds can take several weeks to develop into infant plants and months to mature to the reproductive age, and a gardener seeking to start harvesting seeds soon will want a more mature plant in the garden now.

Harvesting From What You Already Have

Most plants give off seed as a means to reproduce, but sometimes it is as easy — or even easier — to propagate a plant from cuttings than to start from seed. There are many examples of such types of plants. Hydrangea is one example. The hydrangea has beautiful, multi-flowered blooms that sit atop woody stems with enormous bright green leaves. This perennial shrub is often used as a larger landscaping feature, and like most flowering plants, it produces seed. However, it is also very easy to grow new plants from the existing plant. By simply weighing a branch down so that it contacts moist soil (placing a brick atop a branch would suffice), it grows roots at the point where it touches the soil. After it establishes itself, the newly rooted portion is ready to cut from the parent plant and move, creating a completely new plant.

Other plants also thrive in this way, though many require or benefit from a substance called a **rooting hormone**, available at most garden centers, which stimulates the plant cutting to grow new roots when in contact with moist soil. Roses are one variety of plant that propagate in this manner. By taking a cutting from a woody portion of the plant, dipping it in the rooting hormone, and then placing it in a sterile growing medium (there are a few conditions, but this is generally the process), the gardener can grow a new rose plant exactly like the parent.

Vining and shooting plants also propagate by cutting rather than starting from seed. In this case, some do not actually present seed at all. These plants are often prehistoric, surviving through the ages. In the natural environment, these plants spread shoots that adapt and grow in the conditions they meet. Many are nuisances as they overtake the indigenous plants and trees in environments where they are not naturally occurring (such as bamboo in many parts of the United States). Regardless, these extremely adaptable, thriving plants are sometimes well suited for harsher environments. There are actually instances of philodendron cuttings that grow for years in water with no fertilization, no soil, and minimal light, making it a desirable office plant.

It is possible to grow many seeding plants via propagation not involving seeds. In this way, the home gardener can collect a sampling of plants (possibly for free) from the gardens of friends and relatives with permission. The gardener can then nurture these cuttings into mature plants, potentially harvesting seed from them for future planting.

Legacy/Heirloom Plants and Seed Exchanging

One of the best qualities of plants is their adaptability. Horticulturists can take different varieties of a type of plant, say the pole bean for example, and crossbreed them, selecting the most desirable offspring to breed to eliminate undesirable qualities and enhance desired traits. Plants can be bred for herbicide resistance, cold or heat tolerance, draught tolerance, and other practical traits. Horticulturists also breed plants selectively for their physical characteristics, like petal shape and size.

The genetic engineering of plants is largely due to the need for easy crops to grow on large tracts of land to feed large quantities of people. Industrialization has prompted this need as smaller, produce-growing farms have given way to larger, farm conglomerates. While this has benefits in cost effectiveness and consistency, among other benefits, it does have its drawbacks.

Most produce, like potatoes and corn, has many varieties. However, only a few are grown commercially for sale and consumption. Genetically engineered to meet the specific needs of the large farm and the mass market, these varieties have significant limitations as well. Horticulturists fear these crops are more susceptible to mass failure as some of the protective traits of the original plants have been lost to the market-desirable traits bred in to them. Relying on a few varieties on a large scale increases the risk that the entire crop will fail. Such a reliance and failure occurred during the Irish Potato Famine when a fungus from Mexico decimated the main staple crop of Ireland at the time. Had the Irish relied on multiple crops, the famine would have been less devastating.

Heirloom plants are the original strains of these plant varieties, free of genetic interference, usually **open pollinated** (pollinated by natural means), or propagated by cutting or grafting. These are the varieties once grown on smaller farms and in home gardens before post-World War II industrialization led away from that lifestyle. They are genetically stable, passed down from one generation to the next in families.

Some of the benefits of heirloom plants are that they are more readily adaptable to the circumstances of the environment they are grown in over generations. They are often pest- and disease-resistant, as well as tolerant to the extremes of their native climate. Genetic engineering often causes plants to lose these traits. In other less industrialized nations, heirloom plants have always been the standard as small farming has continued as a normal, natural way of life. In the past decade, heirloom plants have seen resurgence in industrialized nations like the United States, Canada, and Great Britain. This is due to the desire to counter crop industrialization, the need to preserve genetic variations that would otherwise fall into extinction, the interest in historical preservation, and familial traditions of passing plant varieties on in family lines.

Heirloom gardening has seen such a large increase in popularity that it is common to find commercial seed distributors selling heirloom varieties. Seed cooperatives called seed exchanges that often cater to the small, organic, and heirloom gardener are increasing in popularity. There are a growing number of these exchanges and smaller swaps in the United States, so much so that the last Saturday in the month of January is now National Seed Swap Day. *Appendix 2 lists many of these exchanges and contact information.*

Larger, organized seed exchanges serve to protect thousands of otherwise threatened garden varieties and distribute seeds to home gardeners interested in growing those plants they aide in preserving. Neighborhoods and communities sometimes assemble their own exchanges, or swaps, at farmers markets and community gardens. Whether it is a large-scale, multi-acre farm that is preserving seeds or an assembly of neighborhood backyard gardeners, they share common goals: Both value heirloom varieties and promote continuing legacy lines of plants.

CASE STUDY:
KATRINA A. PFAFF

Horticulturist/seed quality manager
Totally Tomatoes
www.totallytomato.com
kpfaff@jungseed.com

Katrina Pfaff has been saving seeds as long as she can remember. "Growing up, my family always had a large garden, and a few of our varieties were seeds that had been passed down through the family over the years. We were always careful to collect the seeds and properly care for them so we would have a crop the next year."

Pfaff said she thinks gardening is in her blood as everyone on her dad's side of the family has a home garden and everyone on her mother's side either had a career in horticulture or was a teacher. She first developed a passion for gardening when she was 3 years old.

"Mom got me gardening when I was 3, and we have the pictures of me planting my first pumpkin seed to prove it!"

As she grew older, she developed of love for growing flowers. Because she did not have the money to purchase flower seeds, she began saving seeds from her flowers that she could use the following growing season. She later joined 4-H Club and took interest in horticultural projects.

"It was not uncommon for me to enter more than 100 different items in the fair in a given year. By the time I was in my teens, I had it down to the point where I was even saving things to develop my own colors of flowers."

Pfaff believes it is important to save seeds for the following reasons:

- Saving seeds preserves genetic qualities. While there are many good things that come out of hybridization, it is important to maintain seed purity, especially if that variety of plant offered several beneficial qualities.

- Saving seed is a gardener's insurance for the future and a way to know that your favorites will always be in your garden. Gardeners will know where the seed came from, what disease problems it may have had while developing, and what (if any) chemicals or fertilizers were applied to it. You have the insider knowledge of knowing what to do to make that seed into a successful plant year after year.

She offers the following suggestions for a well-rounded garden:

1. Select the crop or crops you wish to grow.

2. Pick out different varieties within that crop, both of types that you know you will like and then maybe a few that you have never tried (like a white carrot or yellow radish or blue corn). Pick out ones with different maturity dates to have a longer season of available fresh produce. Keep it colorful, too — more color equals more health benefits.

3. When ready to harvest, try each variety individually. If you like it, keep it on the list to grow again.

While some say that Pfaff is old fashioned, and it may be more economical to purchase seeds from a retailer instead of saving them each season, she is an avid believer in saving seeds. "I love what I do. I get to go to work every day and do my hobby. I get to help people and share my love of seeds and horticulture with them. And, hopefully, I get them to enjoy it a little more too."

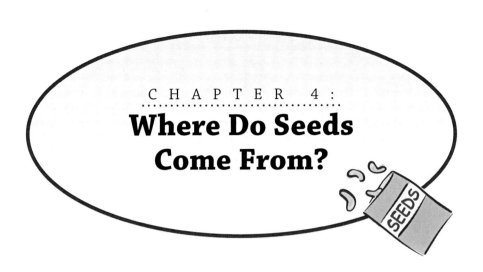

CHAPTER 4:

Where Do Seeds Come From?

Now that you know some of the places seed supplies come from, it is time to look at the original seed source: the plant. Learning how to save your own seeds from the garden is your ultimate goal, and you need to know a few things about plants first. Plants have a reproductive life cycle like all living things. They are born, mature, reproduce, and die. Characteristics and traits from parent plants are present in their offspring with few exceptions. Like any other life form, plants adapt to their surroundings and strive to reproduce to ensure their own species' survival.

The reproductive life of a plant can be a little complicated. There are lots of anatomical differences (and strange similarities) between plants and animals. Not all plants mature in the same way, some taking years to reach sexual maturity and some taking mere weeks. Maturation is not the only thing that differs from plant to plant; how it is pollinated, develops a seed, and disperses the seed differs as well. These differences can mean success or failure to a gardener, as attempting to harvest seed too early or missing the seed by harvesting too late can cost precious time and money. Being able to properly harvest seed ensures gardening success.

The Sexuality of Plants

Knowing how the plant actually reproduces is critical to harvesting the seed from it. As you now know, plants, like any other living organism, have a reproductive life in addition to the other functions (food, ornamentation, and production) they serve. Plants are conceived, grow, and reproduce, though not in the conventional courting and mating style of mobile organisms. Because plants are largely stationary, they rely on vectors, or transmitters, to do the fertilizing for them.

Most flowering plants are hermaphrodites. The biological definition of **hermaphrodite** is an organism, such as an earthworm or plant, which normally has both the male and female sex organs. Being a hermaphrodite means that a plant can function as both mother and father, producing **perfect flowers** that each contain both ovules and pollen, which are the necessary components of plant reproduction. Just as in animal reproduction where the egg needs fertilization from sperm, plant ovules must fertilize with pollen in a process called **pollination.**

Though the majority of plants have perfect flowers, some plants do have flowers that separately contain either pollen or eggs, called **imperfect flowers**. These types of plants are still both male and female, but contain individual anatomy to serve each purpose. Corn, for example, has pollen-producing tassels, as well as egg-producing flowers that eventually become ears. Plants with both male (**staminate**) and female (**pistillate**) flowers are called **monoecious plants**.

Reproduction

Regardless of whether the plant contains male and female flowers separately or pollen- and ovule-containing single flowers, the hermaphrodite plant generally requires no mate for reproduction, just an opportunity to pollinate. Some exceptions to this rule are plants that have perfect flowers that are self-sterile. There must be two flowers in order for self-sterile flowers to pollinate, and two separate plants for **self-incompatible plants** (where all the flowers on the plant are sterile to each other). The pollination of two distinct parents (whether separate flowers on one plant or separate plants altogether) is **cross-pollination**, also called **outbreeding**.

In plants that are not self-sterile, despite being theoretically capable of fertilizing themselves (called **selfing** or **autogamy**, a form of inbreeding), this pollination can still only be accomplished by outside means. Other inbreeding can occur when plants from the same ancestral line pollinate each other, called **biparental inbreeding**. Because the parent plants share ancestry, introducing no variations into their genetics, the offspring plant maintains the same characteristics of its parents. This inbreeding is possible in self-fertile and self-sterile plants.

Though most plants are hermaphrodites, not all are. Plants that are singularly male or female must rely on each other for reproduction, much like humans and animals do. These are called **dioecious plants** and contain only staminate or pistillate flowers. The female plant produces an egg-bearing flower, and the male plant produces the pollen. However, pollination must still occur by an outside means, which is still considered crossbreeding.

Many plants can actually clone themselves. Any plant that can be grown by rooting or planting a cutting from a parent plant is a cloning plant. Plants can multiply their roots (or bulbs or corms), which then divide and grow into individual plants like tulips and hostas are capable of doing. Plants like philodendron and ivy are vines, and new plants produce when the rooted vines separate from the parent plant. Some plants root where broken, mature wood comes in contact with a growing medium (soil), as is the case with hydrangeas. Another type of clone is the potato plant that is grown from cut sections of the parent root, which is also capable of multiplying itself.

Pollination

In order for pollination to occur, the pollen must reach the egg of the plant by a vector. Sometimes this happens when a bee brushes the pollen onto the egg after picking it up or when the wind is strong enough to blow the pollen around in the air, becoming trapped inside a blossom. While the wind pollinates some plants, and in some aquatic plants, the water is a vector, insects fertilize most plants. Pollination that occurs because of the wind or water is called **abiotic pollination**. Conversely, pollination that happens because of insects or animals, including humans, is **biotic pollination**.

Because insects are the main vectors for most flowering plants, these plants develop sophisticated ways of attracting the pollinators to ensure they can reproduce. Blossoms that are fragrant and brightly colored attract a variety of insects. The blossoms provide food via nectar to the insects as a lure, and the insects inadvertently spread the sticky pollen around from plant to plant while feasting.

Pollen is a powdery (usually yellowish) substance that contains the male gametophytes needed to produce the sperm that will eventually fertilize an egg. Pollen lands on the pistil of a compatible plant, activating it. This becomes a pollen tube that delivers the sperm into the ovary and ovule. Once there, the ovule is fertilized, and the seed begins its development.

Seed Anatomy

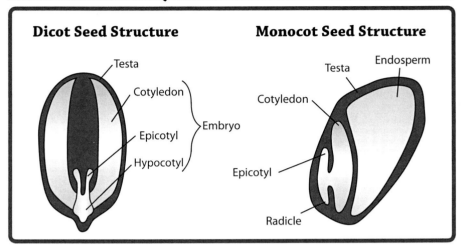

Dicot Seed Structure

Testa
Cotyledon
Epicotyl
Hypocotyl
Embryo

Monocot Seed Structure

Testa
Endosperm
Cotyledon
Epicotyl
Radicle

There are three basic components of a typical seed. Think of a seed in relation to a chicken's egg, which has a shell, white, and yolk. The seed has a seed coat (**testa**), a nutrient supply, and an embryo. The usual innermost of these, the embryo, is an immature plant that will grow and prosper under a combination of time, temperature, moisture, nutrition, and lighting.

Horticulturists assign seed characterizations by the number of seed leaves, or **cotyledons**, contained in the seed's embryo. In a **monocotyledon** (or monocot) **seed**, there is one seed leaf. In **dicotyledons** (dicots), there are usually two seed leaves. Both are forms of **angiosperms**, or flowering plants. Angiosperm means "enclosed seed." These are seeds produced inside of a hard or fleshy structure, or fruit. Some fruits have both hard and fleshy structures.

Gymnosperms, the other form of seed-bearing plant, usually contain two or more seed leaves. Gymnosperm means "naked seed" because there is no special protective structure as it develops. Initially, gymnosperm seeds develop on the outside bracts of cones and some bracts eventually develop cone scales that cover the seeds as the cone develops.

Knowing the characterization of a seed can help a gardener develop those certain conditions the seed will need to grow. Similar seeds are produced in related groups of plants (families) and require similar conditions to germinate.

In addition to cotyledon(s), the seed embryo contains a **radicle**, which develops as a seed root and eventually becomes the root system for the mature plant. The radicle is part of the **hypocotyl**, which is the lower part of the embryonic stem. The shoot that protrudes from the embryo is called a **plumule**, which is the part of the embryo that develops into the main stem of the mature plant and is located at the **epicotyls**, or upper part of the embryonic stem. These are the two points of growth for the seed embryo. The **seed coat** is a protective layer around the inner parts of the seed that develops from the maternal tissue that initially surrounded the ovule. It varies in color, thickness, and texture from seed to seed, but the overall function is the same. It protects the embryo and nutrients when the seed is most vulnerable — the early stages of life.

The structure of the seed nutrients can vary dramatically from species to species. Depending on whether the seed contains an **endosperm** (the tissue that contains the nutrients and that is produced about the time of fertilization in angiosperms), a seed is termed **albuminous** (with an endosperm) or **exalbuminous** (without an endosperm). Some examples of albuminous seeds are grasses, beans, grains, and corn, all of which have endosperms. Those seeds appearing to have no endosperm at maturity, like the pea, squash, and walnut, have simply already absorbed it, transferring all the endosperm's nutrients and energy into the seed leaves.

Many seeds also have other features that distinguish them and serve various purposes. The arils on some seeds prove attractive to birds, which helps disperse the seeds. **Arils** are fruit-like structures, but not actually fruit (false fruit). Birds eat and digest the false fruit and carry the seed until it is defecated where it may stand a better chance of germinating. **Elaiosomes**, similar to arils, prove equally attractive to ants. These are seed appendages that are primarily fat and protein. Ants take the seeds to their larva to feed on the elaiosomes. Once the fatty, fleshy appendage is gone, the ants take the remaining seed portion to their waste area, which is rich in nutrients for a growing seed to capitalize on. Still other seeds, like those of the maple tree, have modified seed coats that act like sails and help disperse the seed in the wind.

Seed Development

In angiosperms, seed development begins with **double fertilization**, which is the joining of a single female gametophyte, or embryo sac, with two male gametes, or sperm, delivered by pollen. In this process, one sperm fertilizes the egg, creating a largely inactive zygote, and the other combines with the large central cell of the embryo sac, making the endosperm develop much more rapidly. The ovary surrounding the newly fertilized ovules will develop into a fruit that protects and aids in seed dispersal.

In gymnosperms, there is also a two-sperm transfer from the pollen, but only one sperm fertilizes an egg. If both sperm manage to fertilize ovules, only one will thrive while the other ovule dies. The surviving ovule will absorb the other during the early stages of development. The gymnosperm seed then is composed of the fertilized embryo and the tissue from the mother plant, which itself will eventually form a cone around the seed.

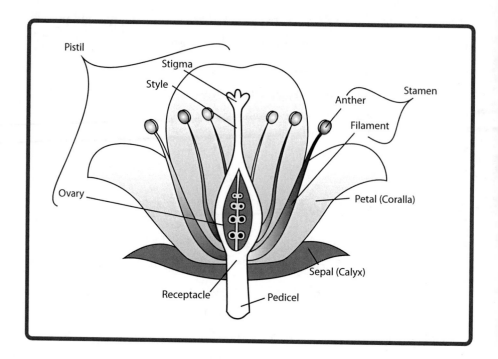

In a flowering plant that has been fertilized, it can be easy to determine the maturity of the seed by the condition of the flower and ovary. Initially, the flower will be in bloom with full petals and alert stamen and stigma. After fertilization, the flower diverts its energy from attracting a pollinator to developing the seed in the ovary. The petals wither and die, and the ovary begins to increase in size. The ovary becomes the seedpod or fruit in which the seed develops.

In the ovary, the seed ripens and develops its tiny root (radicle) and shoot (plumule) that it uses to collect nutrients from the ovary to store in the seed to use upon germination. The ovary swells as the seeds inside grow. The seeds are near maturity when the ovary reaches its full size. As the ovary begins to change color in preparation for its end, the seeds are developing their protective seed coat.

In many fruit-bearing plants, this is the stage at which the fruit becomes ripe and ready to eat. By being eaten, or by other means, the seeds of the ripened fruit are ready for dispersal, to prepare to germinate, and begin the cycle again.

Look for these key indicators to know when seeds are ready for harvesting:

▸ The fruit has stopped growing and is beginning to decline.

▸ The seedpods are hard and cracked.

▸ Seedpods rattle when they are shaken.

▸ The fruit has fallen from the plant.

Types of Seed Dispersal

Dandelions disperse their seeds by anemochory.

Seeds are dispersed in many different ways. **Anemochory** is seed dispersal that occurs by wind. Maple, pine, orchids, and dandelions all have special adaptations that allow wind to assist in seed dispersal. Maple and pine have appendages to the seed coat that are similar to wings, providing lift. Orchid seeds are very fine, like dust, and easily swept away in the wind. Dandelions have bristly tops that serve almost like helicopter propellers to carry them in the wind.

Hydrochory is dispersal made possible by water. Certain plants produce buoyant seeds, and these plants rely on water current to carry the seeds to optimal growing locations. Such seeds are often termed "drift seeds." **Zoochory** is a third means of seed dispersal where animals carry the parent plant to the location where the seed will germinate. This happens in various ways. The seed may have an adaptation, such as a barb, that hooks onto an animal that physically carries the seed to its growing place. Sometimes an attractive, fleshy fruit coating encases the seed, enticing an animal to eat the fruit and later defecate the seed unharmed in a location where it will thrive (along with fertilizer). Seeds an animal harvests for later consumption may never meet their doom as dinner and instead will grow where they were carried and stored. Of course, there is also human assistance, which this text serves to assist. Finally, there is **myrmecochory**, which is dispersing seeds by ants. Ants find the fatty elaiosomes irresistible and the seed portion, which is inedible to them, very resistible. They discard the seed, and it thrives.

Variety is the Seed of Life

Seeds vary in size and shape, from the dust-like orchid seed that numbers in the millions of seeds per gram to the coco de mer, or Sea Coconut, that can weigh an astounding 40-plus pounds, takes several years to mature, and is shaped like two giant, conjoined, black kidney beans. Generally, the smaller the seed, the quicker it is to ripen and disperse. Plants with shorter life cycles (annuals) tend to produce more and smaller seeds, helping to ensure some viable seeds from year to year. Perennials tend to produce fewer, larger, more individually viable seeds, as is the case with woody plants like roses and trees.

Seed coloration also varies. In the bean family alone, seeds cover the spectrum from black to white, with many shades of red, green, brown, and yellows in between. Corn comes in all shades of whites, yellows, reds, purples, and black.

There are many differences in seeds that can throw an inexperienced gardener off. Instead of seed color, size, or shape, the gardener should look for signs of seed ripeness in the entire plant as discussed in the seed development section of this chapter. When seed is ready for harvesting, the entire plant will give off indications that it is time. In this way, the home gardener can optimize seed harvests.

CHAPTER 5 :

Choosing the Right Seed

Understanding the principles of plant sexuality will help you select the specific plants from which to start collecting and saving seed. When selecting from plants that are inbreeding capable because of their hermaphroditic nature, often both parents are closely related. If you planted a row of pea seeds from the same parent plant in your garden, chances are good that fertilization will be a result of inbreeding. The traits of the singular parent plant will be passed on to the successive generation, with the possible exception of hybrid plants, which are covered later in this chapter.

Even though these plants are capable of inbreeding, hermaphrodite plants often are cross-pollinated and not inbred. Experienced gardeners and horticulturists know that the genetic conditions of many plants that inbreed deteriorate after several successive generations (called **depression**), and in order to prevent this depression, multiple strains or families of the same species should be planted and cross-pollinated to promote some genetic variation. If you are looking for fail-proof seed preservation, it is easy to identify the best specimens from your inbreeding plants and save the seeds from these plants.

Saving seeds from specific cross-pollinating, or outbreeding, plants of separate sexes becomes trickier as pollination for these plants is often random. Just because a particular vegetable looks beautiful and tastes delicious does not necessarily mean that seeds from that plant will produce a similar yield. Undesirable characteristics from the father plant might overshadow the characteristics that are desirable from the mother plant. This is the case even if the parent plants are hermaphroditic, as long as they are not closely related. For instance, the mother plant could be the reason that the melon looks great, but the father plant might be the reason that it does not taste very delicious.

In dioecious plants, both parents carry dominant and recessive genes. The dominant genes are demonstrated in the plant you see, but the recessive genes may manifest in its offspring or further generations. Because you are dealing with the product of a plant that comes from completely separate mother and father plants, there is a lower likelihood that the qualities you are trying to reproduce will appear in the offspring. The element of unpredictability means the gardener may — or may not — find a pleasant surprise experimenting with these types of plants.

A Caution about Hybrids

Hybridized plants often carry difficulties for the home gardener. The mule, which is a hybrid of a horse and donkey, is a sterile offspring (all males are sterile and most females are as well). The only way to get another mule is to breed another horse and donkey together. Many hybrid plants share the same shortcomings. Much like the mule, corn hybrids are largely sterile.

Additionally, the genetic coding in hybrid plants is largely unstable. Generally bred for the qualities represented in the first generation after crossbreeding, these often are not present in subsequent generations. The most desirable traits are usually those from the pure (heirloom, even) parent plants. In such cases, it is wiser to collect seed from these and leave the hybridized plants to the commercial grower and mass market.

There are many cautions against saving seeds from hybrids. There is a possibility of positive benefits, but more often than not, it is simply not the case. Experimenting for the sake of experimenting is just fine, but if the gardener would like a consistent yield, hybrids carry a great risk.

Garden Journaling

When monitoring plants for characteristics you would like to see in plants in successive years, it is a good idea to keep a garden journal. Waiting until the fall to decide which seeds to save is a little like buying a book with just the last page. You know how the plant ends, but what did it have to do to get there? Was it the hardest to fertilize? Did it require the most pruning to keep the plant in shape? Was it a delight or a problem child? Did it have a high yield, or was it lower producing in quantity with high-quality taste?

Starting when you sow the seed, record the plant's performance. Photograph it, and note its strengths and weaknesses. If you are looking for the best fruit and vegetables, judging the plant solely by the fruit is acceptable. Most gardeners, though, enjoy gardening for all its therapeutic qualities and want plants that perform throughout the year, not just on the plate. These gardeners journal their plants and wisely consult the journal when selecting seeds they would like to propagate.

To create your garden journal, use a small notebook and chronologically record the daily tasks you perform in the garden. You could also use a calendar to do the same. Make note of when and where you order seeds, when you plant seeds, when they sprout, when you transplant, when the plant provides a harvest, when you prune, how much watering you do, and anything that will help in the following years.

Example of entries can be: "Lots of bees in the garden today," "Noticed 15 sprouts in my rows of beans," "First peas are ready to harvest for food," or "Seed heads on lettuce ready to break open." These are all things that would be helpful to know in future growing seasons.

Plant Qualities

There are many qualities a plant is capable of producing to varying degrees. What follows are some things to consider recording in a garden journal regarding plant qualities.

▶ The number of seeds of a species you planted and how many of those germinated. This will help you estimate projected yield.

▶ The health of the plant throughout its life cycle. Is it spindly as a seedling? Are the roots weak and the leaves as robust as they should be? All these factors provide insight as to whether the plant is getting maximum nutrition to produce maximum results.

▶ Record the time in days it takes the plant to germinate, sprout, produce flowers, and begin to show signs of developing its own seed. Record the rainfall and additional watering, as well temperatures throughout the cycle.

▶ Record whether the plant was plagued by insects or disease. Did it require fungicidal treatment? How bountiful was the produce or how many cut flowers did the plant yield?

▶ Consider factors like storage life, disease resistance, timeliness in blooming and seeding, aromatic appeal and coloration of flowers, insect resistance, and any other factors important for the offspring to meet your particular desires.

Once you decide which plants you may be interested in harvesting for next year's seed, research them a little more, and determine if you will need to pollinate them or if open pollination will be sufficient to carry the seed's line on. Look for how isolated the plant must be and how susceptible it is to cross-pollination. If it is a species commonly grown in your area, it may require special measures (for example, isolation by space or time) to ensure a good seed product.

CASE STUDY: POLLINATION, PRESERVATION, AND ORGANIZATION

Lillian Brummet
Conscious Discussions
Radio host and writer
lbrummet@yahoo.com
www.brummet.ca.

Lillian Brummet is the radio host of her talk show *Conscious Discussions* and a freelance writer for a diversity of topics. She has also written several books on subjects ranging from the environment to marketing and a narrative with poetry. She and her husband have been members of Seeds of Diversity Canada for 22 years and saving seeds for 20 years.

Brummet's interest in gardening and saving seeds resulted from her mother's passion for backyard gardening and research. Brummet grew up on a five-acre farm in the city of Kelowna in British Colombia, Canada. Brummet pursued her curiosity for plant life and took over her mother's seed collection when she retired. "I loved the idea of saving a variety from extinction, helping it to survive generations of neglect," she said. Brummet passed the seed collection on to seed exchange sites, women's resource centers, charity, friends, family, and coworkers. She wanted to make certain the legacy of her mother was sustained.

Since then, Brummet has gardened in a variety of conditions and locations ranging from Okanagan to the boundary regions of British Colombia. She and her husband produce their own open-pollinated, non-hybrid produce using biodynamic, organic methods.

Brummet said she considers pests, pollinators, nutrients, and microbiological activity when planting and saving seeds. She begins the process by growing healthy soil that will supply nutrients to the plants. "Nutrient-rich plants require less maintenance due to a reduced need for foliar feeding, fertilizing, and other special treatments," she said. Brummet warns that ill or weak plants send out a chemical calling card that makes them more attractive to pests.

She said that open pollinating her plants provides a large gene pool of disease-resistant and environmentally compatible traits to help her plants thrive in varied climates and soil conditions, and pollution. Because most plants are pollinated by the wind, Brummet cautions gardeners about the possible contamination of organic plants if chemically altered plants contribute to their pollination.

Regardless, Brummet has not had trouble pollinating her plants. She accredits this to her planting method. "We interplant many different species in one bed and surround the property with plants that attract pollinators," she said. Each of her beds has at least three and as many as seven different types of flowering plants ranging from herbs to ground covers or tall spikes — providing habitat and food for a wide range of pollinators. She also encourages pollinators by providing water for insects and birds to drink and shrubs and vines for shelter.

Mold, disease, insect infestation, and weeds can also concern gardeners. During the germination process, Brummet suggests preventing mold growth by using black plastic mulch or dry grass trimmings to prevent the plants from touching the soil. She also said that watering can be used for disease control, but is often doing the opposite for most planters. "Overhead watering splashes water on the soil, thrusting it up on the plants. Stems and leaves can be contaminated in this way," Brummet said. She recommends using a soaker hose to release water slowly, allowing organics in the soil to soak up the water. Brummet said that a soaker hose or drip lines could also be used to prevent the growth of weeds, which are often caused by watering pathways. Mulch and simply pulling the weeds by hand can also help tackle this problem.

She also advises gardeners to avoid touching the plants after they have been watered. "Handling plants when wet can also transfer the acids on our hands to the plant cells and create all kinds of issues," Brummet said.

Most of her problems, however, can be averted by the natural world. "Biodiversity in the yard will take care of most pest issues. We rarely have an overpopulation of any one critter," she said.

Once her seeds are healthy and ready to be stored, Brummet uses yogurt and other soft plastic containers as seed tags to identify and name her seedlings each year. She cuts them into strips, tapers one of the ends, and marks the top of each strip using a dark, weatherproof pen.

"I also make a note of it in the garden plan sheet," she said. Her husband designed a basic diagram of their garden area. Every year, Brummet marks each variety that she has planted in the proper location on the diagram. "This is helpful in case the tags get lost or memory fails, but it is also helpful for planning succession crops and practicing crop rotation from year to year," Brummet said.

She feels it is important to start saving seeds now, because plants have the possibility to provide future generations with a plethora of advancements in all aspects of life. "We have no idea what kind of benefits, medically speaking, these endangered plants may have. How do we know if a particular variety may hold our only hope of dealing with acid rain or global warming? We could already have lost the cure for cancer without even knowing it," she said.

Brummet recommends the following additional resources for passionate seed savers:

Seeds of Diversity: **www.seeds.ca**

Salt Spring Seeds: **www.saltspringseeds.com**

Trash Talk by Dave and Lillian Brummet

For more information, please visit Lillian and Dave Brummet's website at **www.brummet.ca**.

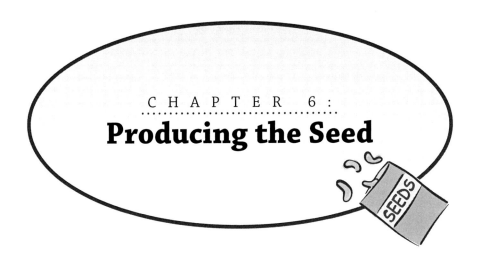

CHAPTER 6:

Producing the Seed

Hand Pollinating

The key to successfully harvesting seeds that will give you the produce you desire is to control pollination. Hand pollination is technically a form of biotic pollination, as humans conduct the pollination. It is not necessary to conduct hand pollination under highly controlled conditions, and it is generally not difficult to execute. It is as natural to the plant as pollination from bees, butterflies, and wasps that frequent the garden.

It is a time-consuming task that does take some attention to detail. For hand pollination to work, make sure the plant is not accidentally (naturally) pollinated by an outside source. Isolate the targeted plant from other plants, and possibly itself (if the flowers are self-sterile, but the plant is not self-incompatible), to keep it from unwanted pollination.

Once the plant is ready for hand pollination, the process is relatively simple. Rub the uncontaminated pollen from a male flower onto the stigma of an uncontaminated female flower. After the pollen transfer is complete, the female flower must remain isolated to prevent further contamination. The hardest part of the entire process is maintaining uncontaminated plants.

Roguing

You can assist controlled breeding using a process that many larger commercial seed growers often use to limit contamination. These growers send workers out into the fields to remove any plants that have inferior qualities prior to the plant's flowering using a process called roguing. **Roguing** is systematically removing potential pollinators that might contribute negatively to the genetic makeup of the harvest.

An at-home gardener maintains a careful balance of quantity and quality to get a large enough yield and a strong foundation for the next year's garden. At home, the gardener cannot always afford to remove every lesser plant as these plants still produce food. You should exercise a careful balance to rogue out significantly flawed plants before they flower, but make sure you still maintain variety and sufficient quantity. This helps further assure that the seed you collect will produce the plants you desire.

Isolation Methods and Techniques

Plants achieve isolation by several means: distance, enclosure (called **mechanical isolation**) to prevent contact with pollinators, or even by time. What works in some gardens for some plants does not work in others for other plants. It is important to know how your plant pollinates to successfully isolate it. While inbreeding plants are capable of self-fertilizing, it is often not the case, and cross-pollination can occur in the open-air environment of a garden.

Out of the four types of pollination available (wind, water, insect, animal), plants generally reproduce using only one form of pollination. Though sometimes there are multiple means of doing so, protecting a plant against the main pollination threat can be sufficient to receive a positive yield. Corn is an example of a crop that is wind pollinated. When the wind blows, it shakes the plant's pollen-containing tassels and the pollen then falls into the silks that protrude from the open tops of the ears. This pollen is very fine and can travel great distances, pollinating neighboring crops. Grasses and grains work similarly, as do some greens. These plants require great isolation distances or other means of isolation in order to be effective. Isolation by distance can dramatically decrease the probability of a crop being fertilized by an undesired neighbor.

Insects tend to be the main pollinators for most plants. Bees are responsible for the majority of insect-delivered pollination, but possible pollinators are flies and some moths. Other insects generally feed on nectar, but are not as significant contributors to pollination as bees because a bee's legs are engineered to serve as pollen vectors. In most cases, bees do not travel great distances from their hives to feed, so distance isolation can play a role. More likely, plants that are insect pollinated are best isolated by time or mechanical means.

Types of mechanical isolation include wrapping single flowers, placing bags over individual plants, or enclosing groups of plants in cages. Entire greenhouses serve for isolation as well, though usually on a commercial level. If using cages or greenhouses, it is possible to introduce natural pollinators like bees into the enclosure to perform the pollination.

Planting one variety of a species as early as possible and avoiding planting another until after the former flowers is a way to use time as an isolation practice. In this way, the pollen from one plant diminishes as the next crop begins to mature. It is a effective method to grow and harvest seeds from multiple varieties of the same fruit or vegetable family without worrying about cross-pollination.

Mechanical Isolation Techniques

Bagging

Bagging is a method of isolating single plants by covering the flowers of the plant, generally in a breathable fabric material like spun polyester or muslin. Gardeners use the bagging method to avoid cross-pollination when self-pollination is desired. It is also used to ensure a flower is not contaminated after it is pollinated.

To bag a plant, use a lightweight material to encase the desired portion of a plant. The enclosure must be able to keep out wind and insects while still allowing light and ventilation to hit the plant. The bag must cover the parts of the plant you want to protect and fit snugly around the stem below. Cotton may serve as a soft, pliable sealant between the bagging and the stem to keep insects from climbing the stem into the bag.

Bagging helps prevent insect pollination and wind pollination to a smaller extent. Many times, the breathable material is unable to keep out the tiniest pollen grains the wind carries. In addition, bagging only protects individual plants or individual flowers on plants.

Caging

Caging carries many of the same limitations of bagging, but multiple plants can be grown inside single structures, increasing genetic variety while still limiting outside influences. Cages are wooden frames with screens or other breathable material wrapping the frame. Gardeners place each cage over a series of plants, using them to either keep pollinators off of a plant, or keep plants exposed to pollinators introduced into the cages.

Alternate-day caging uses two to four cages covering similar, easily cross-pollinated plants like cabbage. The plants all remain covered by their cages overnight. The gardener removes the cage from one variety of plant each day, covering it again at night. This repeats daily, with only one plant variety being uncovered at a time to limit cross-pollination. This is only effective in conjunction with distance isolation because if the gardener next door is growing cabbage as well, your efforts will likely be spoiled by pollen from those plants.

There are a few drawbacks to caging. Without daily pollination, seed yield will invariably be lower, and less fertilization equates to lower seed yields. Cages also compromise light quality as the screens and fabric can significantly decrease exposure to sunlight. This can be a great problem in areas where the growing season is already short.

Taping

Certain plants like squashes and melons have flowers that reproduce best when hand pollinated. Because the flowers grow on vines and not stems, they are less conducive to bagging just based on their structure alone. These plants have male or female flowers, with the females bearing the fruit being significantly outnumbered by the males. The female flowers are precious commodities and the gardener must monitor the flowers for signs they are about to open. Caging is too uninvolved for these plants, as they cannot all be pollinated at once on one day. Alternate day caging means flowers that open inside cages on caged days may miss their pollination opportunity.

Taping is ideal in these instances. Using small amounts of low-tack masking tape, scour the vines for about-to-bloom female flowers and tape them shut, closing out the plant's natural pollinators. Tape shut the corresponding, about-to-open male flowers as well to prevent other pollen from mixing. This is a gentle process, requiring finesse to avoid damage to the flower petals or internal parts. Generally, tape just the outermost tips of the petals shut using a piece of tape wider than the flower and doubled over the top of it. In this way, you can pinch both sides of the folded tape closed and not have to squeeze the flower at all. Generally, you should tape a few males for every female flower you want to pollinate.

When it is time to hand-pollinate (usually in the early morning immediately after you have taped the flowers shut), remove the tape from a male flower first, pull off its petals, and expose its anthers where the pollen exists. Then open the female, pollinate it by rubbing the anther on the stigma, and immediately tape it shut again. Once the female is suitably pollinated by lots of males, leave the flower taped shut for good. The tape will not inhibit the fruit's growth and will fall away from the plant with the withered flower.

Marking Your Territory

There is nothing worse than painstakingly going through the process of selecting your specimens for seed and then getting to harvest time to find you have accidentally eaten what you intended to save or that someone has plucked the prettiest flower in the garden. Be diligent about placing markers in your garden. Use stakes to identify the plants in general and tie colored strings around the stems of those you intend to harvest for seed. In addition to making sure your specimens are not accidentally pruned, plucked, or pulled, these strings can help you make sure you do not miss anything at harvest time.

Special Considerations

Each type of plant — annual, perennial, and biennial — has a special set of considerations for harvesting seed. Because of this, some plants require special considerations and adaptations to ensure their survivability over the winter seasons so they may survive into seed-producing plants. Others have a one-year growing cycle, and the gardener only has one chance to get it right. The following are the major considerations to make when preparing a plant to produce seed.

Annuals

Black-eyed Susan

Gardeners sow annuals from seed at the beginning of their growing season each year. Unlike biennials and perennials, annuals do not survive the winter season, and they go from seed to seed in a single growing season. Because of the nature of annuals, the only planning that exists is how many of them to grow in the year and where. Many annuals are self-seeding and will reappear in varying quantities from year to year.

Gardeners who are intent on harvesting seed from annuals in their garden should also look at plant proximity. Are these plants close enough together to develop seed? Is there sufficient pollination to ensure good seed set so the plants continue to reappear each year, or will the gardener have to aid the pollination process and harvest seed by hand? Will the gardener want to grow more of this particular plant and be able to harvest enough seed to do so next year? They should also take great care to rogue out undesirable varieties that can have a negative impact on the harvest.

Biennials

Geranium

When it comes to seed preservation, biennials often require special care to ensure proper development. Starting a biennial at the right time in the spring or summer is critical to ensuring the plant reaches the right stage of maturity as it goes into its dormancy. If the plant has not developed properly, it can die over winter, even if every other measure is taken to care for it.

Biennials can be grown in two manners: seed-to-seed or seed-to-root-to-seed. These are distinct growing philosophies that are somewhat choice and somewhat a result of the natural environment. In either case, there are requirements that must be met to ensure the plant survives the dormant season.

In the **seed-to-seed method**, gardeners sow the seed in the spring of the plant's first growing season. It is tended and prepared for **overwintering**, which means spending the winter season in the ground. In its second year of growth, it reaches reproductive maturity and develops seeds for harvest at the end of the season. Some seeds grown seed-to-seed need to be planted later in the first year, but they are the exception, not the rule. If a plant does require that special attention, this book notes it in the section for the plant.

Preparing a plant to overwinter can mean mulching it for insulation, setting it under a cold frame or cloche, or wrapping it loosely in burlap. All these measures allow a plant to store its own heat closely around itself so that it does not succumb to cold extremes. *Cold frames and cloches are described later in this chapter.*

When a plant requires the **seed-to-root-to-seed method**, usually when there are harsher winters or when chosen by the gardener, they must be dug up, prepared, and stored at optimal conditions to survive the winter. One advantage this method has over the seed-to-seed method is that when the plants are all dug up, the gardener has the opportunity to further rogue. The very best plants go back into the ground for the second season to produce seeds.

Storage methods over the winter vary widely, but most plants require very low temperatures and high humidity (between 80 and 90 percent usually) in a dark place. Root cellars are optimal, but sheds or garages with the right equipment work well also.

Perennials

Clematis

Knowing the specific requirements for the plants in your garden will save you money and time, as you will not have to replace plants that failed unnecessarily. Many of the special considerations for perennials involve how to help the plant make it through the winter. Like many biennials, especially in colder winter areas, perennials require special care for overwintering. However, perennials do have some valuable characteristics that reward the hard work. For one thing, they produce the same results every year: vegetation and seed.

Some perennials, like hosta and lilac, begin to develop their flowers on shoots long before hibernating. If the gardener prunes them late in the growing season, these plants lose their ability to flower the next year. Other perennials, including roses, must be pruned back before the end of the growing season to prepare for hibernation. Perennial grasses also require cutting, but completely removing dry, dead blades is detrimental to the plant, as they should be left to insulate the plant.

Overwintering

Special tools and techniques exist at the gardener's disposal — greenhouses, cold frames, cloches, mulch, and other insulation techniques, along with root cellars and other refrigeration units — in order to see your plants through their dormant periods and into production for another year.

Greenhouses

There are numerous types of portable, easily assembled greenhouse kits available. Finding a greenhouse manufacturer is as easy as going on the Internet and searching for what your plants need. The pricing for these greenhouse kits ranges from the simple ($500 or less) to the more elaborate (more than $5,000). Advance Greenhouses (**http://advancegreenhouses.com**) and Charley's Greenhouse and Garden (**www.charleysgreenhouse.com**) are just two of the many reputable dealers that offer a vast selection not only of kit greenhouses, but also gardening accessories to go along with them.

If your budget allows, having access to one of these small plastic or glass wonders will bring you hours of gardening pleasure that would otherwise have to wait until after the dangers of last frost pass. However, if you are not willing or able to spend hundreds or thousands of dollars, it is possible to come up with your own version of a portable greenhouse or incorporate an exceptional architectural feature into your garden for a fraction of the cost of the commercial varieties.

If you are not already familiar with salvage yards, now is the time to visit one of these fascinating places. Salvage experts travel to demolition sites and retrieve the discarded materials of old historic houses and buildings. They collect old doors, windows, and antique hardware of all shapes and sizes. If you or someone you know is the slightest bit handy with a hammer and nails, for a fraction of the cost of a newly constructed greenhouse, you can put together a perfectly charming, completely original "shabby chic" greenhouse constructed from an assortment of old doors and/or windows. The big box hardware stores such as Home Depot and Lowe's have detailed plans for do-it-yourself greenhouses in their how-to book sections, and with a little imagination, you can incorporate your vintage doors and windows into a practical, functioning, and unique addition to your garden.

Using cold frames and cloches

If you decide not to add a greenhouse to your garden, there are many other options for protecting your seeds and plants. Using old-fashioned cold frames and gardening cloches is another way you can shelter your seeds and plants. A cold frame resembles old windows that have been put together to form a box in which to keep tender, young plants. It differs from a greenhouse in that a greenhouse fits the plants and the gardener, where a cold frame just surrounds and protects the plants alone. A simple cold frame can protect seeds and seedlings, and extend the gardening season in both spring and fall. A cloche looks something like a large glass bell that is placed over one or more plants as protection against the elements. Gardening cloches are rather old fashioned, but serve their purpose exceedingly well, and the traditional glass ones are a charming, decorative touch among the plants in your garden.

Cold frames

 Cold frames will give you the upper hand against geographical temperature restraints and are a simple, effective, and economical way to start seeds and plants outdoors, and to help protect those plants that are overwintering in the ground. Cold frames have been used in the garden for many years. They are simplistic, old-fashioned, and often overlooked by home gardeners. Just because something is old fashioned does not necessarily mean that it cannot function effectively. They work very well and, depending on the area in which you are gardening, can be a perfect tool for extending the life of your plants both at the beginning of life and in the critical hibernation periods.

Cold frames are easy enough to construct. A cold frame is a four-sided, hinged, slant-topped frame constructed of wood and glass that prevents new seedlings from being damaged or destroyed by cold temperatures and the elements outdoors. Ideally, a cold frame should be constructed so that the sun's rays will strike the glass at a 90-degree angle. The dimensions of a cold frame can be whatever works for you, but keep in mind that the wider the top is, the harder it will be to open and manage once it is open, unless you have a way to keep it propped open.

Length is a personal preference, but most gardeners will recommend the longer it is, the better, as it protects the most plants possible.

A cold frame should always be situated so its opening faces south and receives as much southern exposure per day as possible. Remember that your plants will essentially be sitting underneath a giant magnifying glass. Depending on the air temperature inside the frame, be sure to take precautions and prop open the cover of the cold frame if need be and possibly even cover it altogether if the sun becomes too hot. Keep in mind that, depending on the intensity of the sun, the internal temperature of a cold frame will always be about 10 to 20 degrees hotter than external temperatures. Most young plants will do better in temperatures of between 60 and 80 degrees, so if it is a warm day, over 80 degrees for instance, and the sun is high and intense, the cold frame should be opened to allow the hot air to escape.

Cold frames should extend partially into the ground as well. Some gardeners prefer to sink the bottom part of the cold frame into an actual hole in the earth, while others simply place the frame on the ground and build the bottom up using some sort of porous, insulating material, such as sphagnum moss or shredded newspaper. On top of this, fill the frame up to the edges with whatever soil mixture you have decided to use and rake through it thoroughly in order to disperse the most oxygen in the dirt. You can either plant seeds or seedlings directly into the soil inside a cold frame or you can place plants in labeled pots or other containers inside so that you can easily move them later.

What method you use is merely a matter of personal preference, climate, and what materials you have readily available. Placing the cold frame on the ground is the preferred method in those zones of the country where there is no threat of the ground freezing at night while using the cold frame (because the soil you have filled it with will freeze even faster than the ground itself). It is easier to emplace a cold frame and fill it than it is to dig a perimeter to bury one into the ground, especially if the ground is still frozen. Putting pots and pallets of plants inside the cold frame is also best when there is no danger of frost for the same reasons — the less insulation, the quicker they freeze.

Cloches

Garden cloches can come in many sizes, shapes, and forms. Also called bell jars, they have traditionally been made of glass and originated in Europe. In historical preservation areas, like Colonial Williamsburg, gardeners still commonly and successfully use them in the home garden. They function primarily as a sort of mini greenhouse, protecting individual or small groups of plants from the rain and frost, filtering light, and maintaining a constant humidity level.

A graceful, glass garden cloche nestled among plants in the garden is undeniably a lovely sight, but half of a plastic jug that allows enough light to filter in can serve the same purpose. The plastic jug is not a proper cloche but rather referred to as a hot jug. Either work well, but the clear cloches are preferable because they offer more light and more visibility.

CHAPTER 7:
Harvesting Mature Seeds

Over several months, in the case of annuals, and years, in the case of biennials, you watched your plants mature, begin the reproductive process, become fertile, and develop seeds. You made your choices, helped them along, and anticipated the day you could gather the fruits of your labor — their seed. Now, this will generally be different for different plants, so you will not be spending hours upon hours toiling over countless seeds. Each plant will have its day, and you will be ready.

In Chapter 4, this book gave general guidelines for determining seed maturity. It differs from plant to plant, but those overall conditions are usually the same. Harvesting too soon will result in weak, undernourished seed. If the early-picked seed has enough energy stores to survive through winter and make it alive to sowing time, it probably will not survive through germination. On the off chance it does germinate, the seedling will start at a disadvantage and may never recover. Waiting as long as possible to harvest seed gives it the best opportunity to develop and reach its full potential.

There are generally three ways plants present their ripened seeds.

▶ The seeds may be part of the crop (corn, beans, wheat) and only require that the seed head be dried before removing the seeds. This can be done on the plant or cut, once the seed is matured, which generally occurs when the seed would be ready to eat and beyond.

▶ Many plants present a ripened fruit. Not all such fruits are edible, but they are fleshy coverings in which the seeds have developed. Fruit should be very ripe when picked to harvest seed from, but not to the point where it decomposes or dries, which can both affect a seed in term of longevity.

▶ Some plants have seedpods that shatter when ripe. A large number of flowers like impatiens and columbine fall into this category, as well as lettuce and onions. These seedpods are considered "shatter prone." As the seed is ready, the seed casings harden and open, dispersing the seed. These plants tend to realize seed maturity in waves over multiple days and need more frequent monitoring during harvesting time.

One common technique for harvesting seed from these shattering-type plants is to use a ventilated paper bag or even a loose-leaf tea bag or coffee filter placed over the seed head and stem. Bundle the end of the filter or one end of the bag around the stem, leaving room for the seed head to move and breathe. Using this technique, the plant still provides nourishment to the seed, and there is a mechanism in place to catch the seed when the plant decides to spontaneously disperse.

Separating the Wheat from the Chaff

Once the seedpods have all been collected, the seeds must be separated out for storage. Properly storing seeds makes sure they are viable into the planting season. There are several steps in the preservation process — extracting, cleaning, drying, labeling and storing, and testing — all of which serve a critical role in caring for the seed so carefully produced.

Extracting

In fruits, extracting the seed is usually a simple process achieved by scraping the seed away from the flesh. Just as many do when preparing to carve a jack-o'-lantern from a pumpkin, most fruits have seeds that are relatively easy to remove. In highly fleshy fruits, rinsing seeds can help remove debris. Soaking some seed, like those from different grasses and grains, is a good way to remove chaff, or waste (the good seeds sink and the chaff floats). Some types of seed require a period of fermentation, which helps rid them of enzymes that otherwise prevent them from growing. **Fermenting** entails soaking the seeds and the plant flesh that surrounds the seeds for a couple days until a foul-smelling film covers the water. Fermentation also helps rid the seeds of certain diseases. Good seeds sink in the fermented mixture, which means you will have a greater likelihood of success when you go to plant the seeds, as the bad ones get poured off with all the other fermented debris.

Cleaning the seeds

The gardener must clean any seeds before storage. Depending on the seed, there are different techniques for cleaning. The goal is to make sure that seeds are free of plant material, debris, and bad seeds (any that are nonviable, broken, split, etc.). Some common techniques for cleaning seed are threshing, winnowing, fanning, hand cleaning, blending, and fermenting (a process described in detail in the tomato and cucumber sections later).

▶ **Threshing** is breaking up plant material (including fruits or pods) and exposing the seeds by stomping, beating, or crushing the seed-containing portions of the plant.

▶ **Winnowing** is separating the plant material from seed with a light wind, letting the wind blow away the lighter debris, leaving only the heavier, clean seed.

▶ With **fanning**, you slowly pour already threshed seeds in need of further cleaning in front of a fan placed near a tarp, with the breeze blowing toward the tarp. The heavy seeds fall onto the tarp while the lightweight plant debris blows farther away. In this method, if you do more than one batch of seeds, flip the tarp in between batches so the seeds do not mix.

▶ **Hand cleaning** is removing of plant debris by hand. While this can be time-consuming, if it is a fruit like an avocado, this is not all that time-consuming.

▶ **Blending** is processing some wet, slimy, or slick seed that grows in fleshy fruits. These seeds can be cleaned by blending the entire fruit in a blender on a lower setting, possibly with a plastic blade. In this process, you add water and skim the debris off the top by slowly pouring it off. Bad seed and debris float to the top and good seed sinks.

Drying seeds for preservation

The higher the moisture content of a seed in storage, the less likely the seed is to germinate when it is planted. Care should be taken to give all seeds ample time to dry before packing them for storage. Humidity of more than 20 percent in storage can be highly detrimental to a seed.

A natural method for safely drying seed is to lay the seed out in the sun to dry. Spread larger seeds over window screening and smaller seeds over old silk screens or other tightly woven fabric stretched over a frame. Set them out in a sunny place where temperatures do not exceed 100 degrees Fahrenheit. Exercise care in monitoring the seeds while they dry as they make attractive food for birds and can be light enough for the wind to carry them off.

Though it is usually sufficient for the home gardener to lay seeds out in the sun or to simply spread harvested seeds on paper napkins or newsprint for a few days to dry out, in cooler and humid climates, gardeners can employ other means of drying seed. Keeping seeds exposed to heat to dry them is a possibility, and 90 degrees is the optimal temperature for drying seeds (depending on the type of seeds you are drying) as this temperature gets them sufficiently dry without over-hardening the seed coat or causing it to crack, damaging the seed. You can immerse a seed in silica gel as this gel absorbs most of the seed's moisture content. If you cannot find silica-type granules, you can also use crystallized cat litter and disposable diapers.

Once thoroughly dried, seeds are ready for storage. Some of the institutions that preserve seeds, like seed banks, store them with precise standards in an attempt to get years of viability in a hibernating seed. Their goal is preserving seeds to store them long term. The goal of the home gardener is to preserve seeds so they are viable for the next year's garden. This requires less exacting control over the environment, but the better the environment is controlled, the higher the potential seed yield is.

Seeds do not simply cease to grow once they mature on a plant. They pass through a period of hibernation, during which the moisture they absorb metabolizes the energy they stored during their development. In this way, the seed prepares itself for germination, awaiting the exact conditions it needs to begin growing again.

Storing seeds

Before the spring or summer planting, store the seed to optimize its use of the energy it has stored up to ensure a satisfactory yield. The two major controls the home gardener should consider are moisture and temperature.

Moisture causes the seed to metabolize its energy stores. One of the best possible ways to store seeds is to make sure they are thoroughly dried, package them in labeled envelopes (include variety, date, and growing information), and store these envelopes in airtight containers that have loose silica gel granules in the container. The silica will hold the moisture indefinitely and the seeds will remain dry.

Temperature control is also extremely important. Dry seeds can tolerate freezing conditions, while fungus, bacteria, and disease cannot. Heat, besides being an incubator for disease, also increases seed metabolism and is just as damaging as moisture. Maintaining seeds in a cool, dark place is a good option, but an even better option is to store them in the refrigerator or freezer. There they can hibernate safely, without even the risk of pestilence.

Given the proper conditions, seeds can be viable for many years, not just one season. In fact, the right combination of temperature and humidity can help the home gardener to grow a few years' worth of many seed varieties from one year's garden.

Testing the seeds

Before the growing season starts, it is wise to do a germination test on stored seeds to determine how well they made it through the hibernation. Remember as a child when you placed beans in a cup with wet paper towels or napkins and watched them miraculously sprout? A germination test is a more controlled version of just that experiment.

Take a sample of the seeds you will be growing. Spread them on a paper towel and loosely roll the paper towel up with the seeds inside. Thoroughly moisten the rolled towel and seeds and place them in a watertight, but not airtight, container. Polyethylene bags are best, but zippered plastic bags work well, though you may have to periodically add water. Make sure to label your seeds and the date the germination test started. Check periodically for sprouting.

Once they sprout, count how many of the seeds sprouted out of how many total were tested. This value is the germination percentage for the batch of seeds. If it is low, you may be wasting valuable space planting the seeds. If the percentage is high, it demonstrates good preservation and a high likelihood the resultant plants will be healthy and have good yields (barring external variables).

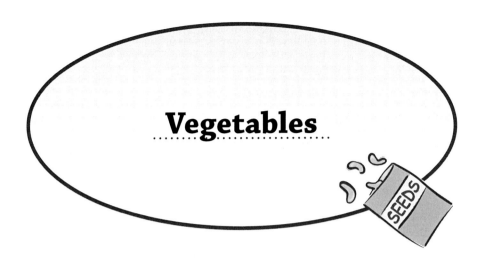

Vegetables

Back in the earlier part of the 20th century, people generally did not simply run out to the local grocery store for the produce that they consumed. Merchants called **greengrocers**, retailers specializing in selling fruits and vegetables on a small scale, were only available to those families who lived in the larger cities. The general stores in the small town, villages, and rural areas carried a very limited inventory of anything that might require any form of refrigerated storage, as that was such an expensive luxury in those days. Those general stores sold fresh potatoes, onions, and other root vegetables alongside jarred and canned goods, but anything else considered perishable was not widely available as it is now.

Consumers knew little about commercial growing at the advent of grocery store chains (in the second half of the 20th century), only becoming consciously aware of organically grown produce and its benefits most recently. Even farm stands did not gain widespread popularity until the past quarter century. Before that, people ate what they grew in their own yards and fields, canning, jarring, drying, and preserving what they could.

Because the average family was larger than it is today, with many more mouths to feed, it was important to till, plow, and plant as much land as possible in order to raise produce for sustenance. Out in the country, aside from field farming grains like wheat, oat, and corn crops as food for both humans and livestock, large gardens planted with every possible fruit and vegetable took up the majority of land on family farms during the early part of this century. For urban dwellers, no city residence was complete without a kitchen garden in the yard.

This all changed around the end of World War II when several developments altered the way Americans obtained, preserved, and stored food. Electric refrigeration allowed homemakers to keep produce fresher for significantly longer. While canning vegetables had been practiced for many years prior to electric refrigeration, freezing them was a new phenomenon. Families purchased large deep freezers for their cellars and back porches. Frozen vegetables grew in popularity so much so that new companies dedicated to growing and packaging frozen peas, green beans, and corn emerged. Considered an indicator of affluence, families served canned and frozen vegetables with pride. As more housewives turned to these new wonders, the backyard garden declined in popularity.

For several decades, the average family in North America rarely consumed truly fresh vegetables, if at all. Besides the frozen variety, canned vegetables had been available for years, and most dinner tables during this time presented either one or the other, or sometimes a combination of the two. The small at-home garden fell out of fashion. At this time, a new generation of housewives emerged, and their new lifestyle did not include growing their own vegetables. They were cooking with canned or frozen produce. It was still considered a sign of wealth and prosperity that a family could afford processed fruits and vegetables.

Americans traveling out of the country during that time discovered to their amazement that restaurants in other cultures still served fresh fruit and vegetables.

European and Asian chefs did not use frozen or canned vegetables. Anyone who has traveled to Europe knows that Europeans buy fresh and consume quickly or simply grow what they eat. They do not keep large quantities of food of any kind for any time.

Chef Alice Waters, from her famous restaurant Chez Panisse in San Francisco, reintroduced America to organic cooking. She set off the "food revolution" of the 1980s, causing Americans to understand once again the differences in the way something fresh from the garden tasted as compared to frozen or canned. The three decades since have brought resurgence in the recognition of and appreciation for good, fresh, wholesome foods that are grown as naturally as possible. Because of this new interest in what they eat and how they get it, more Americans are educating themselves in the ways of their forefathers and learning how to maintain their own gardens so that they can experience the freshest and most nutritious produce available.

Of all the plants that you can grow, vegetables have to be some of the most gratifying. The very idea of burying some tiny seeds with earth and just a few short weeks later being able to slice into a big, beautiful, juicy tomato overshadows any amount of effort the task requires. Vegetable plants, for the most part, are relatively easy to grow. They do not require the pruning, mulching, and fertilizing that many trees, flowers, and shrubs do. Compared to fruit trees, which can take up to a year to bear produce, vegetables bear a product in a relatively short period of time, sometimes just a few short weeks.

In even the smallest of gardens, it is possible to grow enough fresh produce in a season to provide the average family's vegetative diet during the summer months. Family gardeners can also freeze, can, or jar their produce at home, giving them food year-round from their own home gardens. Gardens provide an abundance of fresh, healthy vegetables, and sometimes they provide more than a family can eat, can, or freeze. In fact, as many gardeners probably know through their own trial and error methods, one single zucchini plant can produce enough zucchini to feed their own family, as well as several others, by the end of the summer.

Because so few vegetables are perennial, most of your vegetable gardening will be in the realm of biennial and annual plants. Most annual plants are easily grown from seed and are just as easy to use for seed extraction and preserving purposes. Think about the boundless list of all the different types of vegetables that exist in the world. Most gardeners have certain favorites and plant them year after year. Saving the seeds from these favorite plants will enable you to grow those particular vegetables from the seeds that they put forth each season. You will be growing the "children" of the plants that you grew the previous year.

Each gardener should be selective in choosing the vegetables he or she will grow. It makes no sense to plant something strictly for the sake of planting it. If it is not used, eaten, sold, or given away to someone who will use or eat it, it is merely taking up space in the garden that could otherwise be used for something else more suitable. With that in mind, think about your family's culinary habits. What do you like to eat, and how do you like to eat it? Some gardeners raise tomatoes for sauce and do not ever eat them fresh, while others grow crops of big beefsteak tomatoes for sandwiches and salads, but would not dream of using them to cook with. Identifying and planting only those vegetables that your family is more likely to consume eliminates wasted space and time.

In the following chart, the life cycle column indicates whether a plant is an annual, biennial, or perennial. With an annual plant, its entire life cycle (sowing, germination, sprouting, maturing, producing flower and seed, and dying) occurs in a single growing season. Biennials generally produce vegetation the first growing season and then must be overwintered and will produce seed the second growing season. Many garden vegetables are biennials. Perennials generally follow the same first year as an annual does, but it hibernates over the nongrowing season and returns the next successive season to produce again. Perennials can last several years.

The seed viability number indicates the number of years the seeds will remain viable with at least a 50 percent germination rate under optimal storage conditions. Remember, this means very low humidity and very cool temperatures for highest viability. If the plant reproduces by vegetative means (cloning), this column will describe how it does so rather than the number of years of viability.

Pollination method indicates the main method by which a plant is pollinated. In most cases, it is not the only method, just the one that naturally occurs for the particular plant.

For each plant, the table indicates whether isolation for pollination is recommended. In the section for each plant throughout this book, you can discover further recommendations for how isolation should be accomplished and when in the plant's reproductive cycle isolation should occur. How to go about pollination for each variety is also covered.

TABLE 1: COMMON VEGETABLE VARIETIES QUICK REFERENCE

Vegetable	Life Cycle	Viability	Pollination	Isolation
Artichoke	Perennial	7	Self	No
Asparagus	Perennial	3	Insect	Yes
Bean, common	Annual	4	Self	Limited
Beet	Biennial	6	Wind	Yes
Broccoli	Annual	5	Insect	Yes
Brussels sprouts	Biennial	5	Insect	Yes
Cabbage	Biennial	4	Insect	Yes
Carrot	Biennial	3	Insect	Yes
Cauliflower	Biennial	5	Insect	Yes
Celery	Biennial	8	Insect	Yes
Chicory (Radicchio)	Biennial	8	Insect	Yes

Vegetable	Life Cycle	Viability	Pollination	Isolation
Chive, common or garlic	Perennial	2	Insect	Yes
Collards, collard greens	Perennial	4	Insect	Yes
Corn, sweet	Annual	1-2	Wind	Yes
Cowpea	Annual	7	Self	Limited
Endive	Biennial	8	Self	Yes
Fava	Annual	6	Self	Yes
Garlic	Annual	Bulbs	N/A	No
Kale	Biennial	4	Insect	Yes
Leek	Biennial	3	Insect	Yes
Lettuce	Annual	3	Self	Limited
Lima bean	Annual	3	Self	Limited
Okra	Annual	2	Self	Limited
Onion	Biennial	2	Insect	Yes
Parsley	Biennial	2	Insect	Yes
Parsnip	Biennial	1-2	Insect	Yes
Pea	Annual	3	Self	Limited
Peanut	Annual	1-2	Self	Limited
Popcorn	Annual	1-2	Wind	Yes
Potato	Annual	Clones	N/A	No
Radish	Annual	5	Insect	Yes
Rhubarb	Perennial	3-8	Insect	No
Rutabaga	Biennial	5	Insect	Yes
Soybean	Annual	3	Self	Limited
Spinach	Annual	5	Wind	Yes
Swiss chard	Biennial	4	Wind	Yes
Turnip	Annual	5	Insect	Yes

Because families of vegetables possess similar reproductive qualities, the following information will present information about vegetables in their respective families.

Amaryllidaceae Family

This family contains various Allium species, including the leek, onions, and garlic. Some of this genus reproduces by seed and others (most of the garlic, shallots, and certain onions) are **multicentric**, meaning they reproduce by enlarging and dividing underground (a type of cloning). The common features of this family are its strong, sulfuric odor, as well as a generally strong flavor with edible bulbs and stems.

Though the flowers of Allium are perfect, they cannot self-pollinate as the anthers of the flower mature and shed pollen days before the stigma are receptive. The plants in the family generally flower over 30 days, which gives plenty of opportunity for cross-pollination, and makes isolation more essential.

TABLE 2: COMMON SPECIES OF THE ALLIUM GENUS

Species	Common name
Ampeloprasum	leek
Cepa	common onion (seed-producing), shallot, multiplier onion, potato onion, topsetting onion
Sativum	garlic, rocambole
Schoenoprasum	common chives
Tuberosum	garlic (Chinese) chives

Isolation: Commercial growers isolate these vegetables by 1 to 3 miles. Caging and alternate day caging for different varieties is effective. Bagging is preferred for hand pollinating different varieties, and possibly the most likely to be successful in the small home garden.

Hand-pollination: This is recommended daily in the late morning for two weeks to 30 days. At least ten flower heads of each variety of allium you intend to collect seed from will need to be pollinated, ideally from ten separate plants. The individual flowers you select can each be crossed against all the others, which will ensure genetic diversity.

Harvesting: As they are biennial, in order to have a proper seed yield, these should be started from seed in the spring and harvested in the winter. True-to-type bulbs (those left after roguing) should be replanted in the following spring and will produce seed in the fall. In warmer climates, it is not necessary to harvest the bulbs for overwinter storing; however, not doing so also eliminates the opportunity to rogue and select the best varieties to return for seed.

Common onions and multiplier onions

Allium cepa is divided into several groups.

▶ The Aggregatum group includes all multicentric onions.

▶ The Proliferum group is composed of the topsetting onions (with bulbils that sprout above ground, usually off of a stem).

▶ The Cepa group contains the seed-bearing biennial varieties of onions.

Onions, which historically date back to at least 3,200 B.C. in Egypt, probably originated in the Middle East. In the United States, they can be grown as far south and north as possible, including Alaska. They are classified as short, intermediate, long, and very long day, based on the amount of sunlight they require during the day to grow properly. Gardeners in some regions can grow long-day varieties in summer months and short-day varieties in cooler months, when daylight hours are shorter.

Isolation of approximately 1 mile is recommended for common onions as all varieties may be cross-pollinated by insects. Bagging and caging work as isolation methods in addition to distance. Hand pollination or insect pollination are both effective as well. Wind, however, is not a significant pollination risk.

A special consideration for onions is that they require a period of rest, without which they will not sprout under any circumstance. After their period of rest, they need a state of dormancy, during which they may begin to grow if the proper conditions arise. The rest period is critical and varies in duration, but all onions have it.

There are at least 200 varieties of onions available for mail order in the United States through a bounty of companies. When harvesting your own from the garden, watch for when the flowers begin to dry and fall away as this is a sign the seed is ripening. Because onion is a shattering type of plant, watch carefully for the seedpods to begin to dry to harvest seeds. A ventilated bag tied over the seed head may be used to catch seed. The seeds fall easily from the pods, and light rubbing can get any stragglers free. Because they are relatively small, they can be sifted free of debris. Keep onion seeds in a cool and dry location that is out of light, as the light aids in the breakdown of the nutrients in the seed.

Leeks

Unlike onions, leeks will produce flower stalks in the second year, regardless of the amount of daily sunlight they are exposed to. The only condition that must be met is a cold dormancy of four to six weeks. Elephant garlic is actually a type of leek.

Leek flowers are perfect, but they are outbreeding. They will not cross with other types of Allium, but do easily cross with other leeks, generally by insects. Just like with onions, a 1-mile isolation radius is recommended. Also, as with onions, hand pollination in combination with bagging, alternate-day caging, and even caging where pollinators are introduced are successful fertilization practices.

Leeks have a sort of natural insurance policy that helps maintain trueness. When overwintered in the soil, they can produce side shoots that serve as clones. Whether the seed from the parent plant is cross-pollinated or not, the shoot remains true and provides another opportunity to produce successful seed.

The seedpods on leeks are not as shatter-ready as those on onions, and therefore less attention is needed to catch leek seeds. They do not separate as easily from the seedpods, so they must be threshed. In this case, rubbing the pods together should be sufficient. Whenever threshing, the gardener should take care to use the least amount of force necessary to avoid damaging the seed. Once dried completely, you can store seeds from leeks as with most other seeds — in as low-moisture and cool an environment as possible.

Chives

Common chives are perennial and will thrive for many years. They look like clumps of onion and have a mild onion flavor. They are generally not preserved as specific heirlooms and, as outbreeders, are usually allowed to openly cross-pollinate by insects. They make an excellent addition to an Allium garden, as they will not cross with other Allium varieties.

Garlic chives or Chinese chives are also outbreeders. They resemble tiny leeks and have a mild garlic flavor rather than a mild onion flavor like the common chives do. Like common chives, they cross with each other but not other Allium plants.

Chives are frost-resistant but not cold hardy and therefore must be dug up and stored in colder climates to be replanted in the spring. Whether overwintered or stored and replanted, both common and garlic chives seed during the spring and summer. Common chives produce a purple flower head and garlic chives flower white. The seedpods shatter easily, so, like onions, they must be carefully observed around harvest time. Keep the dry seeds in an airtight container (to keep out moisture) in a cool place, like a pantry, cellar, or refrigerator.

Garlic and rocambole (serpent garlic)

Garlic, though not a seeding plant, has growing similarities to onions and other Allium plants. It requires a period of rest before dormancy and has similar odor and flavor qualities. Rocambole is a type of garlic that shoots serpentine stalks up as it grows. It is otherwise similar to regular garlic varieties.

Garlic is different in that it is a cold-weather plant and, in many cases, can actually grow during the winter. Planted in the fall, garlic is ready to harvest when the tops dry some and bend over. It is cured (dried) before storing for food or future growth. When replanting garlic, the cloves in the bulb are separated and planted individually in the fall, each forming a new head of garlic.

Assuming it has been stored at a cool temperature, a single head of garlic from the grocery store can be grown into up to 20 individual heads of garlic in one year. In two years' time, one original garlic head can provide a family with a year's supply, and it takes minimal investment in time or real estate. Because it does not require any care for pollination, you can ignore them most of the time and still yield a good garlic harvest every year.

Brassicaceae Family

Brassicaceae is a very large and significant family to the home gardener. Many of the greens grown in the home garden come from this family of vegetables. This family was once referred to as the Cruciferae as the seedlings all had four petals formed in a cross pattern. Modern etymology dictates the use of the name Brassicaceae, however, and in the garden, this family includes several genus and species with countless varieties and potential crosses.

TABLE 3: COMMON SPECIES OF THE BRASSICACEAE FAMILY, BY GENUS

Armoracia	
Rusticana	horseradish
Brassica	
Hirta	white-flowered mustard
Juncea	Indian mustard, mustard greens
Napus	rutabaga, Siberian kale, rape
Nigra	black mustard
Oleracea	broccoli, Brussels sprouts, cabbage, cauliflower, collards, kale, kohlrabi
Rapa	turnip, broccoli raab, Chinese cabbage, Chinese mustard
Crambe	
Maritima	sea kale
Eruca	
Sativa	roquette, arugula
Lepidium	
Mayenii	maca
Sativum	garden cress
Raphanus	
Sativus	radish
Rorippa	
Microphylla	large leaf watercress
Nasturtium	watercress

Isolation and pollination notes: This family, with all its genus and species, poses one major difficulty to the gardener: Within each species, all varieties can cross with one another. This means broccoli and cauliflower can cross-pollinate, as could cabbage and kale. As the Brassicaceae family contains a large portion of the produce grown in a garden, this drawback is significant. A lot must be done to prevent unwanted cross-pollination.

This difficulty is compounded further by the fact that, though all the plants contain perfect flowers, all but a few cannot self-pollinate. In fruit trees, the flowers are self-sterile but multiple flowers on the same tree can cross-pollinate. In this family, they are completely self-incompatible and require pollen from an entirely separate plant to cross-pollinate.

Across the species, maintaining isolation of at least ½ mile between crossable varieties and alternate-day caging are the best means of pollination control. Caging significantly limits pollination, which also restricts seed production. Beginning seed savers may only want to use one variety per genus in the growing season, taking care to make sure there are no others in the half mile surrounding their garden.

Harvesting seed: With all Brassicaceae, the seedpods must grow to full maturity on the living plant. They cannot be harvested and later ripened (as corn can). Seedpods present as dry and brown when mature, and are prone to shattering. There are usually multiple pods extending on a stalk upward, and the lowest of these ripens first. So, if the first ripe pod has shattered before harvesting, the gardener can expect the next ones to be ready to catch soon after.

As the plants' seedpods are shatter prone, the seeds are also quite easy to remove from their pods. They do not require any additional special treatment before storage. When storing the seeds, place them at the usual low temperature and humidity level.

Broccoli

Broccoli is a biennial, generally self-incompatible, outbreeding plant. As such, it relies on insects to cross-pollinate. At least two plants are needed to fertilize broccoli, but it is recommended that six or more be used to pollinate in order to maintain a strong, diverse genetic baseline and stable yields.

Broccoli produces seed in the second year or season of growth. When a broccoli plant is being targeted to harvest for seed, it should not be harvested for food even though the consumable portion grows in the first season. Though cutting out the central head may still allow side shoots to go to seed, these generally produce seed of inferior quality.

The broccoli plants produce seed stalks in excess of 2 feet with seedpods running up the stalks. Lower pods ripen first and, like the rest of the family, are subject to shattering. The pods must remain on the stalk on the plant in order to ripen successfully. They cannot be harvested and later ripened (as corn can). Seedpods appear dry and brown when mature. There are usually multiple pods extending on a stalk upward, and the lowest of these ripens first. So, if the first ripe pod has shattered before harvesting, the gardener can expect the next ones to be ready to catch soon after.

As the plants' seedpods are shatter prone, the seeds are also quite easy to remove from their pods. They do not require any additional special treatment before storage. When storing the seeds, maintain them at the usual low temperature and humidity levels that benefit most seeds in storage.

Cauliflower

 Cauliflower shares many of the same qualities as broccoli. It is also biennial, self-incompatible, and outbreeding. Like the rest of its family, cauliflower benefits from isolation practices in pollination due to its susceptibility to cross-pollination. Though both cauliflower and broccoli require **vernalization** (exposure to cold temperatures over a few weeks) in order to flower, cauliflower does not thrive in extreme cold winter regions whereas broccoli may survive.

Apply the same methods of pollination, harvesting, preparing, and drying cauliflower seeds as you would broccoli seeds.

Kale and collard greens

Kale makes a wonderful winter garden plant and is often used as an ornamental as much as it is a vegetable. It is very cold hardy and fades in the sunlight. Collards, on the other hand, thrive on sunlight and do not overwinter as well as kale.

Unlike many other biennials, a benefit to kale and collards is that the gardener can harvest many leaves from these plants in the first year of growth without damaging the plant's potential to develop seeds in the second year.

The seed stalks on these plants grow in excess of 5 feet and are prolific flowerers. Just like the rest of the family, they have shattering seedpods that are best harvested manually over the course of days.

Cabbage

Weighing in as the fourth most-produced plant in the United States, cabbage is commonly classified by growing seasons. Jersey Wakefield is an early cabbage. Early cabbages are sown March through June throughout their growing regions. Late cabbages, like those commonly used in sauerkraut, are sown beginning in May. Cabbages grow best in areas with milder summers, and require storage over winters where temperatures dip below 28 degrees.

Cabbage can go to seed on its own volition, but cutting a shallow X in the top of the tightly bound leafy head will assist the stalks in sprouting. Without an X in the top of the head, the stalk actually painstakingly pushes the head open, unfurling it before it can begin to mature.

Chinese cabbage, Chinese mustard, turnips, and broccoli raab

All four of these varieties belong to *brassica rapa*, a species of the Brassicaceae family. They fit well into the family because like most other plants in this family, they require short-term exposure to cold weather to achieve flowers that can be cross-pollinated to produce seed. They also require the typical one-mile isolation to prevent inadvertent cross-pollination, or at least alternate-day caging. They are biennial with perfect, self-incompatible flowers.

Chinese cabbage and Chinese mustard require protection or digging up for overwintering, as they are not exceptionally cold hardy. They seed similarly to the rest of the family with stalks producing shatter-prone seedpods that must ripen on the live plant. Turnips and broccoli raab are only slightly different in that their seedpods turn a lighter tan when ripening, versus the browns other brassica achieve.

Rutabaga

Rutabaga is a cooler climate vegetable and does not fare well in areas where the summer climate is regularly hotter than 75 degrees. They are inbreeders, capable of self-pollination and easily cross-pollinated. Rutabagas occasionally may cross-pollinate with some turnips and other related species, so isolation of 1 mile is extremely important, and caging is recommended if more than one rutabaga or turnip variety is grown in the same area.

As they are extremely cold hardy, rutabagas are also frost tolerant, and these biennials can overwinter in the ground with proper mulching. Like all the other Brassicaceae, the seedpods ripen and shatter in a wave, so daily harvesting or catching is necessary to get a good seed harvest.

Radish

Radishes should be grown in every garden as they open pollinate, but do not cross with anything other than other radishes. Isolation by distance, which is generally ½ mile in the case of radishes, is enough to protect them from unwanted pollination when only growing one variety. If the home gardener prefers more varieties of radish in their garden, then alternate-day caging is a good option to prevent crossbreeding.

Although the radish itself cannot be eaten without affecting the plant's ability to produce seed, the green, unripened seedpods can be eaten. These vegetables are a popular choice in Indian cuisine. Once they begin to ripen, like the turnip, the seedpod turns tan. To harvest seeds, wait until seeds and the stalk are dry. Radish seedpods are less prone to shattering, and often harder to harvest seeds from.

Turnip

Gardeners grow turnips for two reasons: They either harvest the roots or the greens for consumption. The root shapes vary widely and have either a white or yellow flesh that is covered in skins that are white, cream, yellow, red, purple, or near black, and either yellow or orange flowers. They are biennials and require fertilization. Seedpods emerge on stalks, mature in waves, and need to ripen on the stock. They are outbreeders and will cross-pollinate with any other member of *brassilica rapa*. *(See Table 3 for a list of b. rapa varieties.)*

Brussels sprouts

Brussels sprouts are biennial plants with an exceptionally long growing season that extends into the winter months. Frost and snow-resilient, they produce edible heads in the first season and seed stalks with flowers during the second. They are self-incompatible and only cross-pollinate, but can do so with any other members of their genus. Horticulturists recommend isolation practice of either distance (at least 1 mile) or time as their growing season is late, in conjunction with alternate-day caging to keep pure varieties.

Like the other members of the family, Brussels sprouts grow on a stalk, and ripen from the bottom up. Unlike the rest of the family, the sprouts themselves are not the seed heads. Harvesting the sprouts does not affect seed productions at all. Instead, the seeds grow on stalks from the top of the sprouts' stem in the second year. These pods resemble those of green beans and are harvested as the seedpods begin to dry on the plant by splitting open the pod and removing the seeds. As with other seeds, storage in a dark, cool, dry place keeps the seeds viable the longest.

Chenopodiaceae Family

Unlike Brassicaceae, with many common characteristics shared between the genus and species that belong to it, the Chenopodiaceae varieties vary significantly. This family includes beets, spinach, and chards, which all have dramatically different tastes and appearances. One thing they all share in common is pollination by the wind.

TABLE 4: COMMON SPECIES OF THE CHENOPODIACEAE FAMILY, BY GENUS

Atriplex	
Hortensis	orach, or mountain spinach
Beta	
Vulgaris	garden beet, sugar beet, mangel, Swiss chard
Chenopodium	
Album	lamb's quarters
Bonus-henricus	Good King Henry
Capitatum	Strawberry blite, blite goosefoot
Quinoa	Quinoa
Spinacea	
Oleracea	Spinach

Isolation and pollination notes: Because the members of the Chenopodiaceae family are wind pollinated, isolating plants is difficult. The superfine pollen granules float easily in the air so they require an isolation distance of up to 5 miles. Though commercial seed growers rely on isolation by using larger-scale production methods like green housing, bagging is an effective option for home gardeners.

Before the plants flower, drive long support stakes into the center of the plant. As the stalks begin to develop for the flowers to open on, they are drawn in to the stake and covered with a large, waxed paper bag. As described in the mechanical isolation section of Chapter 6, wrapping the bases of the seed stalks in cotton with the bag cinched at the cotton makes a tight, non-damaging seal to keep out unwanted insects and stray pollen.

Unlike other bagged plants, these bags do not need to be removed for hand-pollination. You can pollinate these plants by placing several seed stalks in one bag and shaking the bag daily. In windy areas, the wind will shake the bag sufficiently, and no attention is needed until it is time to remove the bags.

Harvesting seed: All but one species (*chenopodium capitatum*) require the seedpods to be fully matured and dry when harvested. If there is a late rainy season that inhibits the seeds from drying, the entire plant can be dug up and dried, with its seeds intact, under shelter. Many of the seeds in the family are thorny or prickly, so take care when harvesting because they can cause a good amount of damage to your fingertips.

Spinach

A unique grower, spinach has some garden characteristics that set it apart from its cousins. **Seed-set**, or how long it takes the plant to set its seeds, is climate driven. Longer days (in terms of the amount of sunlight an area receives), repetitive temperature fluctuations, and overcrowding cause spinach to **bolt to seed**, meaning they seed earlier than is normal or desired for optimal harvesting.

Spinach is a dioecious, or single sex per plant, annual. There are male flowering plants that produce pollen and female flowering plants that maintain the ovules and develop seed. The superfine pollen can travel up to 10 miles, giving spinach one of the largest isolation distances of any plant. When caging spinach, the recommended ratios are one male to two females, with at least two males and four females in a caging situation, preferably more. This helps maintain good diversity and health in succeeding generations.

The gardener can harvest the outer spinach leaves for consumption, and the plant will still produce seed and will produce more leaves for harvest. Seed harvesting should come once the seeds are dry on the plant. The wrinkled leaf varieties of spinach have relatively smooth seeds, while the smooth leaf varieties have very prickly seeds. At harvest time, using gloves, grasp the seed stalk below the seeds and strip the seeds from the stalk, catching them in a container. If they are dry, they are ready to store. Almost dry seeds should be left to dry fully (not in direct sunlight as it can burn the seeds) for several days.

Quinoa

 Though not a native to North America, quinoa is a popular import to grocery stores serving Latin American populations and is enjoyed in the same dishes as spinach. Its seeds are harvested and soaked before being used in hot cereal or as a thickener in stews. It is an annual like spinach but is often grown at higher altitudes with shorter day lengths. Quinoa is drought tolerant, making it a good choice for growers in the Rocky Mountain region with modifications (like sowing indoors early). Unlike spinach, quinoa has perfect flowers and can cross-pollinate by insects or wind.

This seed was vital for the Inca population and was regarded as sacred. The Inca's king ceremoniously planted the first quinoa seed of the season with a golden spade. The mature, golden brown seedpods of the quinoa ripen atop stalks of leafy greens. Once they are almost fully dry on the stalks, the seeds can be harvested, cleaned, and dried for storage. After harvesting, the seed stalks should be laid in the shade to completely dry before threshing the seed heads to release the seeds.

Beets

The beet family is quite large and diverse, containing beets used for livestock feed (forage or mangel beets), table beets, sugar beets — which supply about half the U.S. sugar supply — and chards — the leafy green edible portion of the beet. Common varieties of beets range from bite size to more than 15 pounds, in variations of six colors.

Beets are biennials and can seed traditionally in the second year, overwintering in the ground in suitable climates (generally with milder winters). Gardeners refer to this as the seed-to-seed method. As the roots are never dug up, this method does not allow the opportunity to rogue and eliminate undesirable types of plants. Conversely, in the seed-to-root-to-seed method, gardeners will dig up the roots, sort them, trim and store them, and replant them in the spring to grow seed stalks the second growing season.

Beet seeds are ready for harvest when they are dried and brown on the stalk. The distinction beets carry from the rest of their family is that their flowers form single seeds fused into clusters of two to five seeds. Breaking them apart with the least amount of force required is an effective way to get single seeds to plant. Using too much force damages the seeds.

Compositae Family

There are more than 20,000 species in the Compositae family, 11 of which grow in the garden as food, including the sunflower, covered in Chapter 10. This robust family includes the common salad basic — lettuces. Many more ornamentals fall in this family than vegetables, but the few food items it has are garden staples.

TABLE 5: COMMON SPECIES OF THE COMPOSITAE FAMILY, BY GENUS

Cichorium	
Endivia	endive, escarole
Intybus	chicory
Cynara	
Scolymus	artichoke
Helianthus	
Tuberosus	Jerusalem artichoke
Lactuca	
Sativa	lettuce, celtuce
Scorzonera	
Hispanica	black salsify
Tragopogon	
Porrifolius	salsify
Pratensis	wild salsify

Isolation and pollination notes: All flowers within the Compositae family are perfect and most are self-compatible. The plants still often benefit from insect pollination, and the self-incompatible plants require insect pollination to thrive on their own. All plants in this family can be successfully isolated and hand pollinated, and routinely roguing the plants to make sure they are true to type will ensure a healthy harvest of seeds for future growth. Caging and alternate-day caging are effective means for pollination control as well.

Seed harvesting: Any plants in the Compositae family that are biennial and bolt to seed the first season are undesirable. Gardeners should take care not to harvest the seed for future growth, though the vegetation is still perfectly fine to consume. Harvest the seeds in this family when they are dry, either directly from the plant or from seed stalks removed by threshing.

Lettuce and celtuce

Lettuce and celtuce seeds are available by mail order from commercial growers or seed exchanges. Lettuce is a simple dietary staple in the United States, with many families enjoying it on a daily basis. Of the six basic types of lettuce — crisphead, butterhead, leaf, stem, Latin, and cos — only Latin lettuce is not widely used in America. The other five serve many different roles in the common American kitchen.

▶ Crisphead is a common salad lettuce, commonly referred to as head lettuce.

▶ Butterheads are also common for salads and have less tightly packed heads.

▶ Cos is another term for romaine lettuce types, also common in salads, particularly the Caesar salad.

▶ Celtuce is stem lettuce, more common in Asian cuisine in America, and it is often cooked.

▶ Leaf lettuces are widely available heirloom lettuces that come in many types and colors. The home cook knows that color is a general indication of the nutritive value of food and the more color in a lettuce leaf, the more nutritious it can be. Thus, leaf lettuces are becoming more popular in mixed salads. Leaf lettuces are also increasingly used in landscape gardens, as their leafy foliage is quite aesthetically pleasing as well.

As an inbreeding annual plant, lettuce is highly desirable in the garden. Unlike so many other varieties of Compositae, the likelihood of accidental or undesired crossing through insect pollination or other means is negligible. Lettuce flowers in heads that contain up to 25 flowers, each of which produce one seed. The flowers all open at once and self-pollinate as their stamen grow up through the pistil tube. In as little as 30 minutes, the flowers are open and then immediately and permanently close. There is little opportunity for accidental crossing, but a small isolation distance of 12 to 25 feet is recommended.

While lettuce is seeding, it is okay to harvest some outer leaves for consumption (it will not affect the quality of seed production), but it is best to use a few separate plants to produce seed and harvest the rest, as the plant uses its energy to reproduce leaves, and this can weaken the seed crop. Some head lettuce, as well as cabbages, require or benefit from assistance. Cut a slit in the top of the head to let seed stalks emerge, or peel away the outer leaves to expose the seed stalks to help prevent them from compacting and causing head rot.

Harvest seed between 12 and 24 days after the flowers appear. They will begin to have a lacy appearance, and the tiny seeds will be visible. While they are still on the plant, shake the seed heads over a paper bag. If the seeds are ripe, they will fall into the bag, but if they do not fall into the bag, try them again later. Carefully pluck the ripened seed heads, rub them between your hands to loosen the remaining seeds, and shake them again over the bag. Sifting the seeds over a superfine mesh is the only effective way to separate the seed from its chaff, as the seeds are light and fine.

Endive and escarole

With perfect flowers, both endive and escarole are inbreeders capable of self-pollination. They are cold hardy and able to withstand frost and extended near-freezing temperatures, which reduces bitterness in the product. As they are easily cross-pollinated within their genus, endive and escarole require isolation of about ½ mile, or caging or bagging in conjunction with hand pollination.

Endive (or escarole, the broad-leaved endive) is planted in the fall in mild winter climates and may produce early leaves. This is relatively harmless and not a consideration for seed quality. However, if the plant sees too many short, cool days in the first growing season, it will bolt to seed early, which is likely to affect offspring quality. Endives can overwinter in the ground with some mulching, but not in areas that expect hard frosts. In such a case, the roots should be dug up and stored for replanting in spring.

Once the flowers set to seed, the gardener should cease watering endive and allow the seed stalks to thoroughly dry before picking the seedpods for storage. The pods can be planted whole or crushed in order to separate the seeds, but care should be taken to do so without damaging the individual seeds.

Artichoke

Artichokes are somewhat of a garden oddity, which is fitting as they look like the oddest plant in many gardens. The artichoke is an inbreeding species with self-sterile flowers. The stamen releases pollen five days before the pistil is receptive, so at any given time during flowering, pollen from newer flowers fertilizes pistil on older flowers. Instead of hand pollination, isolation, and all the other special requirements for controlled pollination, generally the largest, tightest, tenderest blooms are harvested for dividing and replanting, thus vegetatively reproducing. This is done because artichoke does not come true from seed. Despite that, bagging can be used on those best-looking flower heads in order to prevent cross-pollination. It still does not mean the next generation of plants will be true-to-type. Often, if all the flowers are left to go to seed, many of the seeds will even produce undesirable weeds that are nothing like their parent plant.

When the flower heads are completely open and begin to show their seed plumes, they should be cut for harvest. Once the flower is dried completely, extract the seeds by bagging the flower in a thick porous fabric bag. Press its base forcefully to allow the down to escape the flower and bag, retaining the heavier seeds behind.

Jerusalem artichoke

It is not from Jerusalem, nor is it an artichoke. Of American origin, this tuberous plant is propagated vegetatively from its root. Bulbous and knobby like ginger, the sunroot, as it is also known, is extremely cold hardy. Once it establishes itself in the garden, it is difficult to eradicate. Nonetheless, it is a vegetable with its place in some gardens.

Chicory (radicchio)

Chicory is less common in the United States than in European countries where it is a salad staple, and people use virtually all of the plant in various dishes. The leafy greens are a bitter salad ingredient, as are the forced sprouts of the plant. Coffee connoisseurs roast and ground the roots and add them to their coffee. Radicchio, or red chicory, is common in Italy and used in the United States by gourmands as garnish or in salads.

The perfect but self-incompatible flowers of chicory require interference to pollinate. Chicories will cross easily with each other and may be cross-pollinated by endive, but chicory will not cross-pollinate endive. Isolation by ½ mile, bagging, taping, and caging are all effective methods of controlling undesired pollination. The gardener can successfully grow one type of endive and one type of chicory and only need to cage the endive. Because chicory is a prolific flowerer, alternate day caging is very successful. Even when caging limits pollination, there are so many flowers that even one in five days of open pollination is effective.

Bagging or taping is also highly effective with chicory. Gardeners who use the bagging method can bag or tape the flowers individually, or bag the whole stalks. The gardener hand-pollinates the flowers in the morning when the flowers open, replacing the bag or tape when they are done, and marking the flowers for harvest. When the flowers begin to fall off, the isolators can be removed.

Follow the same process for collecting seed from chicory, as you would do to collect seeds from endive. Once the flowers set to seed, stop watering chicory and allow the seed stalks to thoroughly dry before picking the seedpods for storage. The pods can be planted whole or crushed to separate the seeds, but crush the seedpods gently to avoid damaging the individual seeds.

Black salsify

Also called scorzonera, black salsify was once more popularly grown in the United States but is now obsolete. It is still available from commercial growers, and has various culinary uses. The root has an oyster-like flavor contained mostly in the skin. It also has black skin, white flesh, and strongly resembles a carrot in size and shape. Young leaves are used in mixed green salads, and shoots from the roots can be prepared like asparagus. It is a versatile biennial that grows perennially in milder climates. It can be eaten in the second or subsequent years after it seeds, so the same plants that are used for seed can later be harvested for food.

As an inbreeding plant, and with commercial growers not distinguishing between specific varieties, seed purity is often hard to obtain. Isolation is required by at least ½ mile if you do have a pure variety to keep. However, black salsify is a weed in some areas, and this can make isolation by distance impossible. Caging is much more successful if the gardener wants to maintain seed purity, but because little deviation exists between varieties, it is often unnecessary. Like lettuce, the gardener of black salsify should just enjoy having a plant that is low maintenance for seed production.

Scorzonera seeds disperse by wind when they are ripe, so harvesting the seeds daily will produce the best yield. Look for the flower bases to begin to flatten as a sign the seeds are almost ready to collect. The seeds require further drying before storing, and when they break, they are sufficiently dry to store.

Salsify

Salsify maintains many of the same qualities as black salsify except that the seeds of salsify are viable for up to four years while black salsify seeds are viable two years. Salsify also differs in that it does not succeed as well as a perennial and should be used either for consumption or seeding, but not both. Otherwise, it serves the same culinary functions and is a simple, perfect, inbreeding biennial. Despite its relative obscurity, several types of salsify are available from seed exchanges and smaller commercialized growers. Seeds from the salsify are harvested in the same way as those of the black salsify.

Leguminosae Family

Beans, beans, and more beans comprise this family. Grains are the only food source that is more common than beans. In every culture and society, beans are significant sources of nutrients. Classified and reclassified based on various criteria, the family as a whole contains beans, peanuts, and edible seeds, some of which develop below ground (called **hypogeal**) and others that develop above ground (called **epigeal**).

TABLE 6: COMMON SPECIES OF THE LEGUMINOSAE FAMILY, BY GENUS

Arachis	
Hypogaea	peanut
Cajanus	
Cajun	pigeon pea
Canavalia	
Ensiformis	jack bean
Gladiata	sword bean
Cicer	
Arietinum	garbanzo, or chickpea
Cyamopsis	
Tetragonolobus	cluster bean
Dolichos	
Lablab	hyacinth bean
Glycine	
Max	soybean
Lens	
Culinaris	lentil bean
Lupinus	
Mutabilis	tarwi

Pachyrhizus	
Ahipa	ahipa
Erosus	jicama, or yam bean
Tuberosis	potato bean, ajipo
Phaseolus	
Acutifolius var. Latifolius	tepary bean
Coccineus	runner bean
Lunatus	lima bean, or butter bean
Vulgaris	kidney bean
Pisum	
Sativum	garden pea (edible pod)
Psophocarpus	
Tetragonolobus	winged bean, asparagus pea
Vicia	
Faba	fava bean
Vigna	
Aconitifolia	moth bean
Angularis	adzuki bean
Mungo	black gram
Radiate	mung bean, or green gram
Umbellate	rice bean
Unguiculata	cowpea, black-eyed pea, yard long bean, or asparagus bean

Isolation and pollination notes: Legumes carry an abundance of similarities among the species of the family, making it very easy to garden the family because gardeners do not have to remember a complex range of characteristics. All reproduce via self-pollinating, perfect flowers, and their stamen shed pollen just before the flowers expose their pistils to receive the pollen. They only require mild wind to shake the pollen to set and fertilize the flower. The flowers are generally visually appealing, but insects tend to avoid flowers in the Leguminosae family.

Because of this, the likelihood of cross-pollination is significantly lower, though still possible.

Isolation is successful by distance or caging when the gardener wants to make sure of a pure seed yield, but as crossing is so minimal in cases where there are other garden flowers for insects to visit, keeping a variety of other pollinating plants and slight isolation (12 to 25 feet) should prevent undesirable crossing. If crossing does occur, it will not be apparent in the crossbred seed. Instead, after the seed is planted, the resultant plants will show signs of crossing, as will their seed, usually in the form of a change in seed coat coloration. It is important to label seed batches by parent plant and to plant seeds from multiple parents in each type so that you can rogue out any crossbred plants and still have plenty to harvest.

Bagging is useful with legumes if you want to ensure pure seed harvests. Because they are self-pollinating, you can carefully place bags on the plants before flowers open and remove them after the seedpods begin to develop. This is the only pollination technique you will need and will not harm the plant. You will need to rogue plants to obtain the best plants possible. Plants that are true-to-type and produce abundantly are best for harvesting. As the plants develop, make sure those with off-type foliage, height, color, shape, or number of flowers are removed, or at least not harvested for seed.

Seed harvesting: It is most desirable to leave the seedpods on the plant until they are completely dried to allow them to obtain the most nutrition from the parent plant as possible, making them more viable for storage. While this is possible in areas with longer growing seasons, in areas more susceptible to frosts, the seedpods will require earlier harvesting called **green harvesting**. While it is less desirable because it reduces the nutrient store in the seeds, the best method for green harvesting is to leave the pods on the plant, dig the entire plant up, and allow it to hang upside down to dry.

When the seedpods are completely dry, they begin to split along the sides and often the seeds rattle inside. Breaking the pods open releases the seeds that are ready for storage. Though time-consuming, splitting the pods open by hand allows for better grading and seed separation. Particularly stubborn seedpods may be gently pounded to loosen the casing and release the seeds.

Bean weevils are a major nuisance to the home garden legume seed crop. Weevils lay eggs in seedpods and the larvae hatch in the seeds when they are planted. The weevils then eat their way out, destroying the crop. The life cycle perpetuates once the infestation begins. Freezing dry seeds for up to a week can eradicate weevils in the saved seeds. Seeds must be dry in order to freeze. Those not thoroughly dry will have moisture inside the seed that expands during freezing, causing cell destruction. Ensure the seeds are in an airtight container before freezing so they will not gather condensation when thawing in the container.

Common bean

There are in excess of 2,000 varieties of common beans available for purchase as seed to grow in the garden. Common beans are all inbreeding plants with perfect flowers. As such, they are all capable of self-pollination. This is the type of legume not commonly insect crossed, and it has an overall low probability of accidental cross-pollination. Gardeners can certainly bag and stimulate the individual flowers to self-pollinate, marking those that will eventually be harvested for seed. Otherwise, physical isolation of a few feet between plants of the same variety is enough to maintain seed purity.

If bagging is not used, labeling each flower's seed crop will allow the gardener to rogue out all inadvertent cross-pollinated species, as well as seed to not use in the future. Because seed coat color is a key indicator of crossing, saving a seed from each batch to compare its offspring to will allow you to determine if crossing occurred. In order for this method to be effective, alternate plants with different colored beans, never planting two of the same color next to each other. Planting different seed batches will ensure some seed purity.

Harvesting the dry beans is best, but if frost is imminent, or there is a large amount of late rainfall, the gardener can dig the entire plant up and hang it upside down in a sheltered place for a couple weeks while the beans continue to develop their nutrient store. Most common beans require little effort to remove from their fully dried seedpods.

Garden pea

The garden pea and edible podded pea are inbreeding plants with perfect, self-pollinating flowers that are believed to pollinate before they ever open. This is another easy plant for the at-home gardener because it requires little more than 50 feet of isolation from any other variety to achieve pure seeds. When other types of flowering plants are available to attract bees, the bees will ignore the peas altogether.

Unlike so many other plants that mature late in the growing season, annual peas mature earlier in the summer. Dedicating some of your garden to the pea plants will help decrease your later-season harvest load. And, like the rest of the legumes, they are easy to harvest and shell by opening the dried seedpod and letting the individual peas (seeds) fall out.

Peanut

Like artichoke, the peanut is a garden oddity. It is perhaps the least likely legume to be cross-pollinated with about 1 to 6 percent of varieties openly cross-pollinated. This is thought to be due to significant anatomic differences between varieties. Some varieties (often the older-known ones) require insect pollination due to these anatomical differences despite being self-compatible and require isolation of about 1 mile. Newer varieties are less prone to insect cross-pollination, but isolation is still a good idea. What is truly unique about the peanut plant is that the plant's fertilized ovary spikes (called **pegs**) grow downward into the ground, forming subterraneous seedpods.

Peanuts are a warmer climate species that cannot be grown in the northernmost United States or cooler regions. They are plants that truly like it hot, requiring nearly six months of warmer weather. Four types of peanuts generally grow in American gardens — Virginia, Valencia, runner, and Spanish. Virginia types are true runners, growing low to the ground and spreading. The other two are more erect plants whose seeds can be immediately planted for germination. The Virginia type's seeds require rest before they will germinate.

At the end of the growing season, peanut plants begin to yellow and wither. This is the optimum time for harvesting peanut seeds. Gardeners pull the entire plant, shake off excess soil, and toss the plants in a pile — peanuts intact — to cure or dry. This takes about two to three weeks, and gardeners will need to make sure the plants are kept free of insects and protected from frost. Once cured, the peanuts can be gently pulled from their pegs.

Pigeon pea

Pigeon peas are enjoyed eaten young, in their green pods, or fully mature and eaten stripped from the pods, akin to kidney or lima beans. Because the plants are so beautiful, Americans use them as flower garden plants as much as they use them in the vegetable garden. They have a mild, pleasant taste, high nutritive quality, and are growing in popularity in American vegetable gardens.

These plants are outbreeding, but self-pollinating. They are difficult for insects to cross-pollinate, as their flowers are too tiny for all but the smallest bees. Nonetheless, isolation of ½ mile is effective against cross-pollination. They are very easy to harvest and shell, just as with the peas, and should be left to dry on the vines until they are ready for picking.

Chickpea

Also known as the garbanzo bean, this bean species is often found in the grocery store in cans, ready to top salads. It is another warm weather-loving member of the bean family, like the peanut and pigeon pea.

Chickpeas are inbreeding with self-pollinating, perfect flowers. As honeybees love their flowers, they should be isolated to avoid cross-pollination. Sufficient radius for isolation is ½ mile, and caging works as well, but they do not cross with other species and are not the most commonly grown variety in many regions. If you grow only one variety and wish to maintain seed purity, check with your immediate neighbors to make sure they are not growing another variety.

Once the plant ceases flowering, stop watering. The seeds will mature and dry with no additional water. If you are in a rainy area, you should pull up the entire plant, shake the soil free, and store it in a sheltered place to continue to dry out. Thresh the plant to shake the seeds free or pluck them by hand, but beware that the malic acid present in the foliage can cause skin irritation.

Cowpea

The black-eyed pea is a common variety of cowpea, popular in the southern United States. Cowpeas cannot be grown in the northernmost regions of the country as they require high germination temperatures and long, warm days to mature. Cowpeas produce a mealy pea that is excellent when stewed. In particular, the black-eyed pea is part of a New Year's traditional meal in southern states and considered to bring good luck to those who eat it.

As inbreeding plants with perfect, self-pollinating flowers, these plants need minimal care to ensure pure seed crops. Limited isolation is usually sufficient, but bagging the specific flowers that seed will be harvested from will guarantee a pure seed product. The bags can be applied just before the flowers open until they set seed. Allow mature seedpods to dry on the plant unless there is danger of frost. If there is danger of frost in your area, dig up the plants and hang them to continue drying in a sheltered place. Once dried, remove the cowpeas from their shells by hand.

Runner bean

This type of perennial legume is grown in gardens in the United States more for its beautiful flowers than for its beans. The flowers are significantly larger than those in the rest of the Leguminosae family, and are often pollinated by bees and even hummingbirds. Bagging select flowers to harvest seeds from is effective. The perfect flowers of the runner bean plant need stimulation to self-pollinate. To do so, gently depress the bottom of each bagged flower — squeezing, but not crushing the flower — to simulate insect movement and enable the flower to fertilize by self-pollination.

At even a light frost, the foliage on runner beans dies back. The (poisonous) tuberous roots overwinter well in the ground in areas where there are no hard freezes, and the plant flowers much earlier in second and subsequent years. The bean pods are ready for harvesting as soon as they are mature and begin to change color but should be left on the vine for as long as possible before frost to allow them to intake the most nutrients possible. Dry pods are easily split by hand, and the large seeds fall out easily.

Lima bean

Interestingly enough, many varieties of lima beans contain a chemical that is poisonous if it is not boiled out of the beans. The varieties available in the United States have lower amounts of the natural compound (*cyanogenic glucoside*) and do not require the special preparation many varieties available in South and Central America need.

Some lima beans (small seed varieties) are annuals, and some (large seed types) are perennials. Both are inbreeding plants and can cross with any other lima bean variety, but not with any other legume. As they are a self-pollinating flower, isolation is successful by bagging and hand-pollination. Pressing gently inward against the flower bases simulates insect activity and is the only stimulation lima bean flowers need to set seed. The nectar of lima beans is highly attractive to honeybees, so to produce pure seed stock, use physical isolation of 1 mile between varieties if not using bagging or caging.

Lima seedpods are prone to shatter easily. When picking the dried pods, enclose them in your hand as you pull them off their vines. If you suspect weevils, pick them before they are dry, and lay them out to dry quickly (using artificial heat like a hair dryer that does not exceed 90 degrees will speed the process). Then freeze the beans for several days to kill the infestation. If weevils do not seem to be an issue, the pods should be left to dry on the plant.

Lentil

Lentils are annual, perfect, inbreeding, and self-pollinating. The plant's tiny flowers can hardly be cross-pollinated by any vector, so these beans need minimal care regarding pollination and isolation. They are not very heat-resilient, nor do they thrive in the northernmost regions of the United States. An interesting note about lentils: Archaeologists at Dumlupinar University in Turkey discovered what they estimated were 4,000-year-old lentil seeds. In April 2010, biologists at the university planted 17 sprouts that grew from the germinated seeds. They are very easy to harvest and shell and are even prone to shattering. Allowing the pods to completely dry on the plant may result in them splitting before you have a chance to harvest them, so pick them just before they are completely dry. Set them aside in a sheltered place to finish drying. You can split them open easily, and the seeds will fall out.

Fava bean

Fava beans are inbreeding and self-compatible, as well as outbreeding and easily cross-pollinated by bees. The recommended isolation distance for favas is 1 mile, or else the gardener must use bagging or caging to ensure seed purity. Unlike most other legumes, the fava is hard to shell. Threshing the dried seed stalks is almost required to harvest any large number of seeds. Despite that, and due to its cold hardiness, it is desirable in northern regions where there are fewer bean types available. In southern regions, it is also desirable because a fall planting produces spring harvest.

Soybean

Soybeans are another garden delight in warmer climates. As the flowers self-pollinate before they ever open, there is little to no danger of cross-pollination in soybeans. Soybeans are sensitive to the amount of light they receive on the average day; so select the right variety for your area to make sure the plants will reach maturity. Too many or too few hours of sunlight can cause the plant to grow improperly or not at all.

There are many uses for soybeans. They are valuable for protein content as well as for their extracted oil. Processed dried seeds are used in soy sauce, raw bean sprouts top salads and sandwiches, and cooked soybeans are included in many stir-fry dishes. An accepted substitution for milk for those who are lactose-intolerant or for vegans is soy milk. Soybeans have excellent nutritive value and are popular in U.S. culinary circles.

However, soybeans are hard on the fingers. Prickly, brittle, dried seedpods may be shelled by hand, but mechanical means are better to prevent damage to the skin. One method is to spread the seeds out on a thick, fibrous cloth like burlap, cover it with similar material, and drag a weight over it (a large, smooth rock will do). Similarly, you could roll it with a rolling pin to crack the pods. Periodically pull the top fabric back and remove the exposed seed. Start with lighter pressure, and gradually increase until you are able to open the pod without crushing the seed.

Tepary bean

These plants are traditional to Southwestern Native Americans. They are used in diets similarly to green beans, shelly beans, or dry beans. These inbreeding annuals are usually safe from crossing as they grow in regions were few pollinating insects are common. Tepary beans thrive in arid, hot conditions, base or alkali soil, and are draught tolerant. They suffocate in cool, wet conditions.

The seeds of the tepary bean harvest easily once they are dried on the plant. Like the common bean, they are easy to shell as well.

Yard long bean

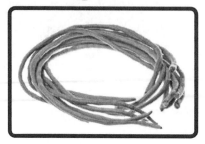

An annual, heat-loving vine, the yard long bean is also a low-maintenance legume. It is self-pollinating as the stamen sheds pollen along receptive pistils before the flower opens. Bees do not find it attractive, and it rarely cross-pollinates. Isolation is not required. Though it can be grown as a food crop in most of the contiguous United States, in the northernmost regions, it will not mature far enough to produce viable seed. After drying on the plant, the seeds of the yard long bean are very easy to shell once they are picked.

Umbelliferae Family

The Umbelliferae family is a major garden presence in American gardens. These plants share common features, but are all distinct as well. One thing that ties the Umbelliferae family is the characteristic umbrella shape of its plant's flowers. These flowers are all referred to as **umbels**. The first flower developed in any single plant is called a primary umbel and contains the largest quantity of seeds of any flowers to follow.

As the plant matures and develops more energy to focus into reproducing, it shoots off a second and third tier containing its secondary and tertiary umbels. These umbels each also develop seed later in the season. Many growers do not wait until the tertiary umbels are mature to harvest the ripe primary and secondary umbels, especially in hotter climates when the heat threatens to damage the crop.

Though some of the Umbelliferae family is toxic, some of plants are delicious food. Some are grown for their roots (like carrots) or roots and foliage (parsley), and others for their foliage alone (dill). Root and root/foliage varieties are biennials, and foliage-only varieties are annuals.

TABLE 7: COMMON SPECIES OF THE UMBELLIFERAE FAMILY, BY GENUS

Apium	
Graveolens	celery, celeriac
Anethum	
Graveolens	dill
Anthriscus	
Cerefolium	chervil
Arracacia	
Xanthorrhiza	Peruvian carrot
Coriandrum	
Sativum	coriander/cilantro
Daucus	
Carota	Queen Anne's lace, wild carrot
Foeniculum	
Vulgare	fennel
Pastinaca	
Sativa	wild parsnip
Petroselinum	
Crispum	parsley, parsley root

Isolation and pollination notes: Though Umbelliferae have perfect flowers, the flowers are self-sterile. The flowers' anthers shed pollen long before the stigmas are capable of being fertilized. Flowers on the same plant can pollinate one another because they open over an extended period. Insects are almost necessary for pollination unless the gardener desires to hand pollinate several tiny flowers. Before you decide to pollinate the plants by hand, understand that each flower should be stimulated daily for up to 30 days, fertilizing at least ten of each variety to ensure good seed diversity. It is not impossible, but it is time-consuming to fertilize enough to get a good seed harvest.

Alternate day caging is a much easier task for Umbelliferae varieties. For it to be successful, plants must still be isolated. Horticulturists recommend 3 miles of isolation for this family. Bagging is also effective for this family, and perhaps preferred. Using a material like gossamer will keep the pollinators from other plants out and still allow you to very gently shift the bag, rub the stamen, and disrupt the pollen to land in some open stigma. The larger the number of plants treated in such a way, the better, as pollination percentages are lower than if openly pollinated.

Harvesting seed: The annual Umbelliferae are generally quick to seed and shatter prone. Harvest seed from the annual varieties when the stem to the seedpod is nearly, but not completely, dry to ensure a better seed crop in terms of quantity and quality.

The biennial varieties are generally grown seed-to-root-to-seed. You should plant seed in the spring garden and allow it to mature into the fall. Dig up the plants to sort, select the best and true-to-type varieties to store, and replant in the spring. These plants flower, fertilize, and develop seed for harvest during the second growing season. In warmer climates, it is possible to plant the biennial's seed in the summer or fall, allowing it to grow through the milder winter. The plant will bolt to seed in the spring.

Collecting umbel seeds is relatively easy although the seeds are somewhat fine and prone to shattering. Just like with annuals, harvest a dried seed head on a nearly dried stalk for best results. Lightly rubbing the umbels over a screen or between the hands separates the seeds from their pods. Sometimes the seeds require further drying, but not often. If they do, laying them out to dry is appropriate as long as it is less than 95 degrees outside, and they are not in direct sun.

Celery and celeriac (celery root)

Celery is a very particular grower. There are several regions in the United States where growing celery is a laborious process. Celeriac is less picky a grower. While celery is grown for its foliage, celeriac is a root vegetable. It grows to about baseball or orange size before harvesting. It is prepared cooked or raw and tastes like milder celery. Celery and celeriac are the same plant, but depending on what you intend to harvest — the leafy stalks or the smooth roots — it is called one thing or the other.

Both celery and celeriac are strong, outbreeding biennials. They will cross with any other variety of their species and with each other. Isolation of 3 miles, caging, or bagging is recommended to keep seeds pure.

Both plants are grown seed-to-root-to-seed in cooler climates and must be dug up, overwintered in cool storage, and replanted in spring. In warmer climates, you can sow early (spring) or late (summer). For plants you intend to sow early, dig the roots in the fall for storage over the winter. This will nurture the plant for seed production, allowing it to save as much of its nutrient as possible. If you have late-sown seed, then overwinter the roots in the ground. This allows the plant to direct its nutrients into growing a stronger root system for the early harvest next year. Whenever time allows, dig up the plants to store them because you can then also rogue out the poorer plants (they are still fine for eating) and save for replanting.

Dill

Dill is a relatively common kitchen herb savored for its dried seeds. It is an annual that does not have a long growing season. You will be collecting dill seeds relatively shortly after you plant it. In warmer climates, it does well in a winter garden for greenery as well. As with the rest of the Umbelliferae family, dill shatters easily when ready to go to seed and should be harvested after the heads are dry but while the umbel's stem is still green.

Because dill has a shorter growing season and can germinate in cool to warm temperatures, it can be grown in intervals throughout the season. In this way, it is possible to grow different varieties without physical isolation. Dill is good for isolating by time.

Coriander or cilantro

Coriander is an outbreeding annual that bolts quickly to seed. As there are few varieties available, cross-pollination is not generally a concern for the home gardener. This is because the few varieties grow in different climates and regions, as well as earlier or later in the season, so they are not a cross-pollination threat. Cooks harvest the foliage for Asian and Mexican dishes, including salsa, and the flavor does not significantly vary from variety to variety.

Just as with dill, coriander (cilantro) has a shorter growing season and can germinate in cool to warm temperatures. It can grow in intervals throughout the season, and it is possible to grow different varieties without physical isolation. This is another plant that is good to isolate using time.

Carrot

Carrots are easy to start from seed, and once they have matured and been harvested, they provide a fascinating way to save and preserve their seeds. Carrots are biennials and are pollinated by insects and other flowering carrots. To maintain seed purity, isolation is useful along with the bagging and caging methods. Many gardeners do not allow their carrots to go to seed, which is also beneficial to controlling cross-pollination. Most home gardeners plant seeds to harvest carrots, and because they never see their second year, they never flower.

One interesting fact about carrots is that both they and the common plant Queen Anne's lace are in the same family and will cross-pollinate. If you are aware of any Queen Anne's lace in the area, you will need to cage or bag your carrots to ensure you are getting pure seed from them. Watch your carrots and discard what look like white roots in your carrots when you dig them up as these are actually examples of the wild Queen Anne's lace.

In order to maintain the attributes of the carrots that you have chosen, you should save the seeds from quite a few plants; 50 or more is a good quantity. The bigger the gene pool, the more likely the carrots that come from their seed will be genetically stable.

Once the plants have gone to seed, harvest the umbels before the stems are completely dry. Carrot seeds are exceptionally fine and the umbels shatter easily, so daily harvesting is essential. Depending on how many carrot plants you have let go to seed, you should only need to collect the seeds from the first set of umbels and perhaps some of the secondary ones that appear on each plant. Keep the umbels indoors for a few days, and then roll them around in your hands or push them through a strainer in order to remove the outer covering. Carrot seeds will easily slip through the holes in the strainer because they are tiny, so be careful not to lose any. Store the carrot seeds in an airtight container in a cool place, as high temperatures can cause the seeds to germinate artificially. If you will be waiting several months before replanting, store them in the refrigerator.

Fennel

Fennel is a diverse herb that is used in cooking, teas, candies, and even eaten raw. In the United States, it occurs in the wild as a weed, and because it is an outbreeding biennial, this can pose a problem for the gardener wishing to save the seeds for purity. There are not many varieties of fennel available from commercial growers, but they can vary significantly in structure and flavor, so isolation is required to get a pure seed harvest. A ½ mile of isolation is sufficient to prevent crossing by insects, and bagging is the preferred method for gardeners looking to grow and produce seed from more than one variety in closer proximity. The seeds are ultra fine and gardeners must take care to prevent them from shattering before harvesting. Pick the umbels of fennel when the stems are still slightly green to avoid this.

Parsnip

Parsnip is a much more cold hardy Umbelliferae member. In fact, freezing ground temperatures can help the root obtain a more desirable flavor. A biennial, parsnip is outbreeding and easily cross-pollinates by insects. Isolating the crop by 1 mile produces sufficient room to prevent cross-pollination, and caging and bagging are effective. Like the rest of the umbels, harvest these seeds before the stalks are completely dried.

Note: Parsnip leaves and stems seep a chemical that is a major skin irritant. Wear protective clothing when harvesting the roots for food or the seeds for preservation. Wash your hands before touching anything else after handling parsnip greens.

Parsley and parsley root

Parsley is an outbreeding perennial whose umbels rely on insects for pollination. Thankfully for parsley, the plant is very attractive to various insects. Of course, this means parsley is easily cross-pollinated with other varieties of its species. Isolation of 1 mile is sufficient to maintain seed purity; bagging or caging will also ensure purity.

Parsley can be overwintered in the ground with dense straw mulching, or it can be dug and stored (preferably planted) indoors. If it is root parsley, it should be dug up to examine and select true-to-type varieties for replanting. Like all other Umbelliferae plants, harvest the extra fine seeds from a dry seed head on a nearly dry stem before the seed heads shatter.

Other Vegetables

All of the vegetables mentioned in this section are parts of larger families, but either deviate significantly from their family members in growing and pollination habits, type, or use, or the rest of the family is not generally grown in the vegetable garden.

Potatoes

Potatoes belong to a family that is otherwise grown for its fruits, the Solanaceae. *The rest of the family is covered extensively in the following Fruits chapter (Chapter 9).* Potatoes require lots of room to grow and spread. They can grow out to 5 or 6 feet in all directions. The more the plant is allowed to spread, the better it produces. Plant your potatoes in rows that are 3 to 4 feet apart to give them plenty of room. It is useful to continue to add soil to the plant as it grows. The plant foliage grows up, and the tuberous roots do as well.

There are two means of producing new potato plants: vegetative cloning and harvesting seeds from a berry produced from a pollinated flower.

▶ Most potatoes that are grown for consumption are grown from tuberous (root) cuttings that self-replicate when planted. They are true-to-type as they are essentially clones. Growing potatoes in this way has its benefits. The potatoes are usually larger when grown vegetatively, and they are predictable. The new plant will be just as the original was if grown under the same circumstances. Of course, it has drawbacks as well. There are tuber-transmitted diseases that cause crops to fail (as did a fungus during the Irish Potato Famine), as well as pests that eat the delicious roots, both of which can be carried to the new plant via an infested cutting.

▶ The other method for reproducing potatoes is to use seeds that come from the berries of the actual potato plant itself. Potato blossoms are inbreeding, but the seeds do not breed true-to-type. Even within a single seedpod, the seeds will individually provide different results. If you are looking to experiment and just enjoy a few surprises, this is the way to go. If you really liked the potatoes you already grew, save a few to cut and replant.

Gardeners will recommend that if you truly are looking to start your potato plants from seed, it is best to purchase your initial seed inventory from a commercial grower. There are more than 700 varieties available for order. The plants will be free from disease, and you can attempt to maintain this disease-free status by using sterile soil and good pest management techniques.

Corn

If you have the room in your garden, growing corn will provide with you and your family with one of the garden's most well-liked and versatile vegetables. Of all the vegetables that we cultivate, corn is the most truly American. The Native Americans first practiced growing corn as a crop, and some historians say that corn is the main reason that most tribes settled in specific areas and became more agricultural than nomadic.

Corn has played an important role in the exploration and settlement of North America. If Native Americans had not introduced the Pilgrims to corn during that first brutal winter at Plymouth Rock, most of them would have died of starvation. It is widely believed that one of the reasons that the Pilgrims survived at all was because they had stockpiled quantities of corn that the Native Americans had generously given to them and taught them how to cultivate.

Along with homegrown tomatoes, fresh sweet corn straight from the garden is one of the hallmarks of summer eating. No matter how you cook it, sweet corn is a delicacy that is hard to resist. Growing corn is not difficult, but it does require more room than most vegetable crops and somewhat more maintenance as corn has a tendency to attract more pests than other crops. When starting out, avoid the packages of hybrid seed corn that are available in the garden centers. You will want to plant seed corn that can be pollinated, and because hybrids are unable to truly reproduce, you should avoid them. Several heirloom varieties will let you grow both white and or yellow sweet corn for the table and for seed and give you excellent yields. Any good garden center or hardware store catering to gardeners should have these seeds.

Stowell's Evergreen and Country Gentleman are two types of heirloom white corn, and Golden Bantam and Golden Midget are two yellow heirloom varieties. To give the corn the best chance of pollinating successfully, plant two to four rows that are alongside each other. Corn should be planted in hills with five to seven seeds in each hill. Once the corn has sprouted and grown 4 to 6 inches tall, thin each hill until you have two to three plants per each hill. Fertilize with a nitrogen-heavy fertilizer periodically and water generously. Corn needs at least six hours of sun exposure each day for the ears to gain size and for the kernels to ripen properly.

Because corn can so easily be cross-pollinated by corn that is as far away as 300 yards, you will need to ensure that the ears of corn from which you plant to save seed are isolated. Check the pollen status of the neighboring crop and take steps so that your corn silk is not in the developing stage as the same time. You can accomplish this by staggering the dates of seed planting. Finally, if you are surrounded by other gardens, quarantine the ears of corn from which you want to save seed. To do this, cover each ear with a nonplastic bag of some sort before the tassels appear. Tassel bags are specifically designed for isolating corn and are ideal because they allow humidity to escape and fresh air (but not wind) in so the plant may continue to thrive. Plastic bags will suffocate the sealed-off portion of the plant.

Check the tassel development of the ears periodically. Once you see the pollen develop on the corn silk on the ears, remove one of the tassels and use it to pollinate all the other ears of corn from which you are planning on saving seed. To make certain that you will have enough seeds from these particular plants, hand pollinate at least 20 corn plants. Leave the bags on until the corn silk turns brown. After removing the bags, you will need to tag each ear of the plant you want to save so it does not get picked when you harvest the rest of the crop.

The ears that you have designated to save should stay on the plant for about a month longer than the other ears that were harvested for eating purposes. They can stay on the plants until the first hard freeze and then taken to a protected location (preferably indoors) for drying. Pull the husks back to provide better air circulation, and hang them up in a cool, dry place. Corn seeds can be saved in this manner each year for the upcoming season. Once the corn has been dried, it will be ready to plant in the spring.

CHAPTER 9:

Fruits

Anyone who has ever had the opportunity to taste fruit that has not been grown in a small garden knows how radically different it tastes from the produce in the big grocery chain stores. In most of the rural areas, there are produce farms where families can pick their own fruit and vegetables for a small fee. This handpicked fruit tastes the way it used to years ago, before mass production methods became the norm. In comparison, how many times have you purchased expensive apples, pears, or peaches in a grocery store only to bring them home and discover they are mealy and tasteless?

To circumvent this problem, you can turn to local farm stands where the quality of the produce for sale can be somewhat, but not necessarily, better. Unless the farm stand owners are growing their own crops or working in cooperation with other farmers, the merchandise in their stands could still be from the same large distributors that sell fruit to your grocery store. Even if you do find a higher standard of fruit and vegetables at local farm stands, the prices can actually be higher, as the smaller businesses must struggle to compete with the larger grocery outlets.

The fact that you have been paying too much money for fruit that you could grow better yourself should give pause for thought. You always have a choice. You can continue buying subpar produce and complain about it, or you can take a leap of faith and begin to raise your own fruit and berries in your own garden. Saving the seeds from your own fruit plants, planting them, and harvesting the fruit from the plants they produce is the ultimate goal in self-sustaining gardens.

Growing Fruit in a Large Garden Setting

In Chapter 1, you learned about how Americans once relied on their gardens for sustenance. Many long hours of backbreaking work were put into the garden, and most of the work was done by hand. Instead of gasoline-powered rotary tillers, men, women, or animals plowed the gardens. There were no "weed whackers," leaf blowers, or power edgers to help tend the garden.

In those days, it was not uncommon for a family to spend entire days for weeks at a time getting the garden prepared for planting. Because those families depended so much on the produce that came from those gardens, there was no questioning that every year the monumental task of cultivating and maintaining a large garden was necessary. As the family grew so much of their food themselves, and the larger the family, the larger their garden was. Everyone pitched in, and even the smallest child would be put to work weeding or picking the vegetables as they ripened.

These days, large gardens are planted and nurtured more as a recreational outlet than for the sake of necessity. In modern times, having access to just about every type of produce nullifies any compulsion to grow one's own fruits and vegetables. Now Americans have gardens as large as they can accommodate, so that they can spend time working at something that they love and look forward to the bounty it will yield at the end of the gardening season.

Fruit in the large garden means room for fruit trees, rows of vine plants like melons, and space to try things that do not fit in a smaller garden setting. You can grow several varieties of each species and experiment with hybrids while still maintaining seed production. Any hybrid plant in the small garden takes room you could use to grow a seed-producing fruit. In the large garden, you have more room to experiment.

Fruit in the Small Garden

Small gardens are for the inventive gardeners out there. Small gardeners must be adaptive and find ways to grow plants in the conditions available. In an apartment with just a patio, for example, the gardener must build a garden in containers, as there is no land. Considerations like drainage and watering come to mind, as it is easier for soil to dry out in a container, and it is easier to drown a plant without proper drainage. These gardeners also have to think vertically instead of horizontally, selecting bushing plants and those that can be vine-trained or trellised over those that grow in rows. Fruit plants that grow in pots are valuable, as they can be hung or wall-mounted to optimize room.

The first plants that come to mind when thinking of what to grow in small spaces are berries and grapes, as the plants are smaller, easy to manage, and can be adapted to containers and smaller settings. While you can grow practically any type of berry in containers, and can create decent-sized hedges out of some of the larger bush types, for general household consumption purposes two varieties stand out. Strawberries and blueberries lend themselves to small garden cultivation very nicely, as both plants can be grown quite successfully in containers.

Apartment dwellers are not the only people confined to small gardens. Those in townhomes, trailers, retirement communities, or just homes with smaller yards are also limited by what plants they can grow. These gardeners must use every spare nook of patios and porches, balconies, and windowsills.

Fruit trees and shrubs in the small garden

If you have had no prior experience growing fruit trees or bushes, the very idea of planting and cultivating either or both of these can be fairly intimidating. If you are intimidated by growing such a large plant, remember that a tree is a plant that requires the same things that any plant needs to grow and flourish: sun, carbon dioxide, oxygen, water, and food.

Example of an apple tree using espalier techniques

While it is true that working in a smaller garden setting does present some challenges in your pursuit, using the technique of espalier will give you options that you never thought you had. **Espalier** is an ancient horticultural and agricultural practice of pruning and training the woody growth of plants to grow flat or straight, like against a wall or on a trellis.

If you have ever perused any seed and nursery catalogs, you are aware several types of trees have been bred as miniature versions. While these smaller cousins of the traditional apple and pear lend themselves perfectly to espalier, practically any fruit tree or bush can be pruned into the easily manageable shape that produces the espalier effect. This practice has been widely used by gardeners in Europe for generations, and the results are not only unique, but quite lovely as well.

 In essence, the trees are pruned into a rather drastic, but decidedly decorative, configuration so that instead of filling out in circumference, they flatten out and grow up the wall or fence upon which they are being trained. While the method of espalier can be done against a supporting outdoor wall, it can also be accomplished using an ordinary fence, thereby giving you space for a tree or shrub on either side. If you use the espalier method to support your plants, those trees and plants must still be maintained to the standards that will keep them as healthy and productive as possible. Proper light, water, and fertilizing will ensure that your trees and vines are cared for in a way that will safeguard their well-being.

Common Fruits

There are countless varieties of fruits the home gardener may grow and enjoy. Many fruits have more in common with garden vegetables than one would think. In fact, many fruits are even legislatively designated as vegetable that are not — tomato and squash, for example. Other fruits have much less in common with vegetables and require drastically different fertilization techniques. The apple for example requires cross-pollination. For the apple and other fruits, without cross-pollination, they do not produce fruit.

Techniques like isolation become murkier with fruits. Though you may want to isolate your trees from crossing with other varieties not to your liking, they must remain open near a hearty supply of pollinators with ample vectors to carry the pollen from one plant to the next. In these cases, work with your neighbors and be critical of which varieties you choose if you plant fruit near theirs.

TABLE 8: COMMON FRUIT VARIETIES QUICK REFERENCE

Fruit	Life Cycle	Viability	Pollination	Isolation
Apple	Perennial	3-6	Insect	No
Blueberry	Perennial	5-8	Insect	No
Cranberries	Annual	5-10	Insect	Yes
Cucumber	Annual	5-10	Insect	Yes
Eggplant	Annual	5	Self	Limited
Pepper	Annual	3	Self	Limited
Pumpkin	Annual	5	Insect	Yes
Strawberries	Perennial	3-6	Self	Limited
Squash, Summer	Annual	5	Insect	Yes
Squash, Winter	Annual	5	Insect	Yes
Tomato	Annual	4-10	Self	Limited

Growing and Preserving Seeds from Berries

Strawberries, blueberries, blackberries, and raspberries can also be started from seed and are some of the most popular fruits in the world. Besides being so easy to eat on their own, these berries can be used in a multitude of recipes and even in making wine. Berry bushes are attractive additions to the garden landscape, and it is a fun activity to grow enough berries for your family's meals.

Once you decide to grow the seeds you have cultivated from your garden, keep the seeds for any of these plants in the freezer for a month before sowing them in the spring, or use natural stratification (exposing the seed to cold temperatures to break the dormancy of the seed), sowing them in the fall. *Stratification is discussed in detail in Chapter 11.* It is wise to plant several bushes of each variety near each other at the same time so that proper pollination can occur.

Blackberry, raspberry, gooseberry, currant, cranberry, and blueberry plants will need to be pruned periodically to keep them from getting out of control and to promote heavier yields. Especially in the case of blackberry and raspberry bushes, use gloves to do this, as they have thorns that can damage your hands. The best time to prune is in the early spring, although you can and should cut away any dead wood any time you notice it, and continuously harvest the fruits to promote new fruit growth.

Ericaceae Family

Ericaceae is an acid-loving family of plants that comprises both fruits and ornamental flowers. There are herbs, shrubs, and trees in what is also called the heath family. The blueberry, cranberry, and huckleberry are fruits that are part of this family, all in the vaccinium genus.

Blueberries and huckleberries

Blueberries are an easy to grow perennial. They will reproduce and return year after year, and a single bush planted in a large enough container will produce plenty of fruit. Blueberry bushes can grow up to 6 feet tall, so even if grown in a container, they still will need room to spread up and out. Blueberries should be grown in direct sunlight and like acidic soil, preferably with a pH between 4.0 and 4.5. They should be pruned in the spring and then again in the summer. By cutting away the dead and woody sections of branch, you will force the plant to expend more energy into the parts of the bush that remain, such as new berries. As much as you might not want to cut back any of the branches, this will force the plant to put forth even bigger berries the following year.

The biggest challenge in growing blueberries is keeping them away from the birds. Birds can strip a blueberry bush clean of berries in a matter of minutes, and no deterrent really keeps them away. Unless you want to spend an inordinate amount of time shooing them away, it is a good idea to keep the bush (or bushes) covered in bird netting once it has started to produce fruit. This allows the bushes to get the light they need, but the birds cannot get at the berries.

Furthermore, although the taller, shrubbier varieties are typically planted as rows of rooted cuttings from a single parent plant, so-called lowbush blueberries are typically produced on naturally occurring barrens where plants can reproduce using fertilizers, burning, and removing competing vegetation.

Flowers of blueberry and huckleberry species growing in the temperate zone are typically white, nodding (or drooping), and urn-shaped to cylindrical. The dimensions of the flowers, especially the depth of the **corolla** (the collective petals of the plant) and the breadth of its opening, often define which bee species can easily reach the **nectaries** (the nectar-secreting organ) and consistently contact the stigma while foraging. All pollinators take nectar from the basal nectaries if they can be reached.

Isolation and pollination notes: Among the kinds of blueberries and huckleberries sought for their edible berries, both the wild species and their cultivated derivatives require insect pollination for fruit production. Pollen is shed through a pair of pores at the tip of each anther. For some reason unknown to biologists, bees intentionally vibrate the blueberry flower, which shakes the pollen from the anthers into the stigma. They do so either by buzzing their flight muscles or drumming the anthers using their legs. Bees that simply probe the flowers for nectar remove little pollen. Some bee species steal nectar through holes that they make (or find) in the side of the flower's corolla. These individuals fail to contact the flower's stigma and fail to transfer any pollen. Instead of picking up pollen from one flower and carrying it to another, this quasi-biotic/quasi-mechanical pollination does not carry risk of cross-pollination, as there is no exchange of pollen. In this way, the inbreeding blueberries are self-fertile and self-pollinate. Blueberries are unusual among cultivated fruits in that cultivars and varieties may only be the result of intentional crosses between two or more species.

Seed harvesting: It is easy to extract the seeds from blueberries. Their thin skin, which makes them such a popular target for birds, also makes for easy seed extraction. Simply put a handful of ripe berries in a blender with a little water. After blending until the skins are broken and the berries are relatively liquefied, let the mixture settle and strain off the pulp. Separate the seeds from the pulp. Set them on paper towels to dry and once they are completely dry, put them in an airtight and watertight container for storing purposes. You can also place the seeds in a labeled paper envelope, place the envelop inside a sealed jar with a tablespoon of silica, and place the jar in the refrigerator.

Cranberries

The American cranberry is a wood-vine perennial that thrives in acidic, sandy bogs, swamps, shorelines, and stream banks of northeastern North America. They enjoy growing near water, and farmers capitalize on this during harvest when the buoyant berries are washed into the water and skimmed from the surface. Along with blueberries and huckleberries, cranberries belong to the heath family. A prolific producer, the cranberry plant produces an estimated 20 million flowers per cultivated acre. Cranberry plants bloom in midsummer, usually June and July, producing short, upright shoots of single flowers.

Cranberries are a strong source of vitamin C and were once carried aboard ships to prevent scurvy in sailors. The plant is also valued for its ability to stay off urinary tract infections.

Isolation and pollination notes: The pendant-like white flowers of the cranberry are perfect. The stigma of the flower's single pistil extends beyond the anther tips, making it unlikely the plant will self-pollinate. Instead, bees probe cranberry flowers for nectar much in the same way as they do blueberries, vibrating the flowers as they harvest their food and causing the pollen to shed through pores at the anther tips. Other attempts at pollinating mechanically fail so farmers rely on bee populations entirely for cranberry pollination. Distance isolation between variations is the only reasonable means of isolation, as unvisited flowers do not generally produce fruit. Any means that segregate the plants from their pollinators reduces harvest.

You will only need a single cranberry plant to successfully pollinate a cranberry plant; however, depression from inbreeding occurs, and over time, the resulting fruits will produce fewer viable seeds. Having a variety of plants in close proximity to each other and having a mixture of seeds in future plantings secure genetic stability in cranberries.

Harvesting: Once they have matured, the tart red cranberries can each contain up to 35 tiny black seeds. To separate the seeds from the flesh, process the fruit in a blender. Once blended and rinsed clean of debris, the seeds can be dried and stored in the same manner as blueberry seeds.

Rosaceae Family

Raspberries, blackberries, dewberries, cloudberries, strawberries, and other related species belong to the Rosaceae, or rose, family. Plants in this family are diverse and widespread, with members growing on every continent aside from Antarctica. Carbon dating of fossilized Rosaceae found in Colorado indicates plants in the family are at least 35 million years old.

To harvest the seeds from these fruits, smash the fruit through a sieve or pulverizing it in a food processor to create a mixture that will float when water is added. When stirred, the seeds sink, and the unwanted debris floats. Pour off the flesh and debris and dry the seeds fully prior to storing them.

Strawberries

Strawberries are a pretty plant with their dark, shiny foliage and delicate white flowers. Even when they are not bearing fruit, they make a decorative addition in your garden. Because they are attractive and will stay green all year long in warmer climates, you might consider using them as a permanent addition to your landscaping. They can go into any conventional type of pot, and do well as long as they have room to spread. Strawberries are prolific growers and their runners will travel out of their pots and onto the ground. As with any crop that offers high yields, be prepared for more strawberries than you ever expected. This is when you can put your canning skills to use or freeze the strawberries for future use.

Although strawberries are technically perennial plants, they begin to deteriorate as they age and produce fewer berries after three or four years. This is a common occurrence in many fruit-bearing vines, which is one reason saving seeds from perennials is as important as saving seeds from annuals. After having grown your own strawberries, you will undoubtedly become accustomed to eating and enjoying them. If you have been saving their seeds, you can readily replace the dying plants with plants you have grown from the seed you have collected.

The traditional terra-cotta strawberry pots are specifically designed to maximize the output of a strawberry plant. The key with these is to stuff them with as many plants as will fit into the holes provided. It might seem like you are overfilling the pot, but just make sure that each plant is surrounded by plenty of potting medium and kept consistently watered and fertilized. Strawberries will thrive in this setup, and you can hang the pots, anchor them to the wall, or secure them to a balcony ledge.

Strawberry pot being used to grow herbs. Photo courtesy of University of Illinois Extension

Once established, strawberries are an exceedingly hardy perennial and will reproduce rapidly. Once the berries start to ripen, you should continuously harvest them. As the plants begin to bear fruit, they slow their production if they carry the fruit. The faster you remove the ripened fruit, the faster the plants will produce more fruit. This principle is the same as deadheading your flowers.

Most strawberries reproduce or propagate by sending out runners, a form of vegetative reproduction. In large garden settings, because of their sprawling growth patterns, strawberries can take up as much room as many of the other crops. Two varieties, Sweetheart and Baron Solemacher, do not propagate by putting out runners, but rather rely on cross-pollination and seed. Because these varieties do not spread, more plants are needed to produce a good yield in the garden.

Strawberries are among the easiest of plants from which to extract seeds. Because they are on the outside of the berry and more accessible, you can either take the time to pick them away from the surface using a toothpick (which is very time-consuming), or you can push the berries through a sieve or pulverize the fruit in a food processor with a plastic blade on low. Once they are crushed, add extra water, and pour off the remaining pulp with the excess water. Retrieve the seeds from the stringy shreds that may still be attached, and put them on ceramic tiles or pizza stones to dry completely. These surfaces work best, as the seeds tend to stick to paper, which is usually used to dry other seeds. You can then store them in a sealed, labeled envelope along with a desiccant and place them in an airtight container in a cool, dark location, ideally the refrigerator.

Before attempting to grow new plants from the seed that you collect, place the seeds in the freezer for a month before sowing, or plant the seeds in the autumn so that they will have to go through the colder temperatures of winter before germinating and sprouting in the spring. *This process — stratification — is covered in detail in Chapter 11.*

Raspberries, thimbleberries, and blackberries

Mature blackberries and young red blackberries

The fruits of raspberries, thimbleberries, and blackberries each contain one or two seeds. Flowers of these plants are perfect, self-fertile, and can be self-pollinating. Though deformed and underdeveloped (also called partial) fruit and fully fertile seeds develop if the flower self-pollinates, there must be a vector to pollinate the shorter stigma to produce a complete fruit. In order to guarantee a successful crop of berries, they need maximum exposure to pollinators. Again, bees are an essential part of a garden with raspberries or other berries in the rose family. Maintaining several plants of the variety you choose to grow also ensures genetic stability and reduces the likelihood of depression in successive generations.

Wild species in the family are sometimes self-fruitful, sometimes self-incompatible. Red raspberries are unique in that they form seeds without fertilization. However, the berry cannot produce fleshy tissue if it is not fertilized.

Harvesting seeds is one way of propagating these plants, but raspberries and blackberries also propagate by vegetative means. They can send out shoots, called suckers, or spread rhizomes, thereby cloning themselves. Clones of these plants maintain the exact genetic makeup of their parent plants. Plants grown from seed may be hybridized.

Raspberry, thimbleberry, and blackberry seeds are exceptionally fine and difficult to separate from the flesh of the fruit. You can harvest seeds from a fully ripened to overripened (but not rotting) fruit. Place the fruits in a very fine mesh sieve, and smash the fruit through the sieve using the back of a spoon or similar tool. Handpick the seeds, and set them on a paper towel or clean newsprint to dry completely before storing in a cool, dry place.

Solanaceae Family

The Solanaceae family is composed of many valuable plant species including the various peppers, potatoes, and tomatoes of the world. Though the plants of the various genus and species vary, the flowers share common attributes. All flowers in the Solanaceae family have five fused petals, forming a disc-shaped flower with five central stamens.

A significant contributor to the dinner table in America, the Solanaceae family, offers more than 2,000 species of plants. This text covers the most prevalent genus and species in the United States, with many more available in Central and South America. Eggplant and tobacco are also members of the family along with many other tomato-like species that make for excellent variety.

A note about Solanaceae: Legislation in the United States dictates that many members of this family are considered vegetables for use and trade. However, they are fruit-bearing plants, and people consume the fruits. They also have more in common with vining fruits like grapes than they do with other vegetables, so they are being included in the fruits section for these reasons. The only exception is the potato, which is not raised for its fruit, but rather the vegetation of the plant.

TABLE 9: COMMON SPECIES OF THE SOLANACEAE FAMILY, BY GENUS

Capsicum	
Annuum	ornamental peppers, chili peppers, cayenne pepper
Pubescens	rocoto
Cyphomandra	
Betacea	tree tomato, or tamarillo
Lycopersicon	
Lycopersicum	garden tomato
Pimpinellifolium	currant tomato
Physalis	
Alkekengi	Chinese lantern
Ixocarpa	tomatillo
Solanum	
Melongena	eggplant
Muricatum	pepino
Quitoense	naranjilla
Tuberosum	Irish potato (covered in the vegetable chapter)

Isolation and pollination notes: Solanaceae are not generally attractive to bees, but are still cross-pollinated by other insects. Isolation and caging are usually necessary to maintain seed purity, but you should harvest seeds from several species in the garden to maintain safe genetic diversity.

Seed harvesting: Harvesting seeds from Solanaceae plants is a fun and messy process, one that children will love. Crush, slice, smash, or otherwise open the fully ripened fruit over a plastic bucket. Add enough water to fully cover the mess and stir the mixture vigorously. The good seeds sink and the skin, pulp, and bad seeds float. Skim off the debris, add a little more water, and stir. Once there is nothing floating, strain the seeds, rinse them, and you are done.

Because there is a slimy coating on many of the seeds, they will stick to paper, so it is better to use other means to dry them. A stoneware baking dish or pizza stone placed in a warm area (but not in direct sun) is ideal for drying Solinaceae seeds. Store the seeds in a labeled package in a dry, dark, cool place while they wait to be sowed.

Peppers

This section covers all varieties of peppers grown in America, both hot and sweet types. Peppers are native to South and Central America, but many varieties thrive in the United States as well. A mild weather perennial, pepper is not frost hardy and should be overwintered indoors or in greenhouses. Pepper plants make excellent choices for container gardening because of their growth habits and growing them in containers makes it easy to move them when it comes time for frost to threaten in cooler climates.

The heat in many peppers comes from the chemical compound capsaicin. The compound is found only in the interior tissue until the fruit ripens, and then it is present in all parts of the fruit, including the seeds. The more cold hardy and thirstier the plant is, the hotter it will taste.

Peppers are inbreeding plants. The flowers of the pepper are perfect and self-compatible, and they are attractive to pollinators. Up to 80 percent of seed from plants that were not isolated results in crossbred plants. Though not detrimental to the first generation of plants, and sometimes resulting in delicious accidents, further generations of the crossbred pepper can produce undesirable characteristics. In varieties that do cross, expect the sweet bell pepper flavor to be lost to hotter peppers because heat is a dominant trait and sweet is recessive.

Isolation is required, but at only 500 feet, to maintain pure seeds. Caging works with one variety per cage and potted plants can be caged (or more effectively bagged) as well. If there are not pollinators in the cage, hand pollinate the plants by tapping the flower at its base.

In most parts of the world, green peppers are not eaten because they are not yet ripened. Fully ripened peppers may be yellow, orange, red, purple, or black. In the United States, people enjoy green peppers cooked and raw, and that is acceptable, but keep in mind green peppers are not ready for harvesting. This is important for the gardener to know because the seeds are not mature until the pepper is fully ripe.

To harvest pepper seeds, you can scrape the seeds off the core with a knife, or you can put the entire pepper or core into a food processor with water and blend it on low until there is pulp and seed. After that, put it in a plastic container with water, stir, and let the good seeds sink.

*Care should be taken with the hotter peppers, like chilies. Do not allow children to handle them, and wear protective gloves when handling them. Also, work in a well-ventilated area or use a protective respirator, particularly if you are sensitive to capsaicin or chili oils.

Pepper seeds are fully dry when they break instead of bending. Once they are dry, store them in a cool, dark, dry place until you are ready to plant them.

Tomatoes

Christopher Columbus brought tomatoes back to his native Spain where they were popular because of their origins in the New World, but they were largely considered poisonous when eaten raw. It was not until people stopped using pewter dishes — tomatoes chemically reacted to that specific alloy, leaching out toxic metal — that they realized tomatoes were not actually poisonous.

All varieties of tomatoes are a beautiful and diverse fruit. It is considered a vegetable and grown in vegetable gardens, used as a vegetable in cooking, and legislatively, it is a vegetable as ruled by the Supreme Court of the United States in *Nix v. Hedden*. However, a tomato is the ripened ovary and seeds of a flowering plant, which technically makes it a fruit or, to be more precise, a berry. This particular fruit comes in various shapes and many colors, with flavors that range from tangy to sweet, and mild to intense. The fruit can be large, as in the case of larger, beefsteak tomatoes, or tiny, like the currant tomato, which is less than ¼ inch in diameter.

Tomatoes are inbreeding plants, like the rest of the Solanaceae. Because their style (pistil) is retracted within the anther (stamen), it is very unlikely the plant will cross-pollinate. However, currant tomatoes have longer styles and do cross more readily. A gardener can maintain a couple varieties of modern tomatoes along with a single currant variety without needing to isolate any tomato varieties. You can include as many varieties of currant tomatoes to your garden as you would like as long as they are isolated using bagging or caging.

When harvesting tomatoes for seed, it is necessary to allow them to ferment to remove the sticky gel that covers the seed, inhibiting germination. Fermenting means leaving the seeds in water in a warm place for a few days until a layer of mold completely covers the surface of the water. This simulates the natural rot a fallen tomato experiences and prepares the seed for drying. As soon as a layer of mold covers the water's surface, strain and rinse the seeds to prepare them for drying as quickly as possible. Tomato seeds tend to want to germinate, so if they are fermenting too long they will germinate. If they take too long to dry, they will germinate as well. As long as the seeds are completely dry, they may be stored in a cool, dry place, preferably in an envelope placed in a glass jar along with a desiccant.

Eggplant

Eggplant and tomato-fruited eggplant are much different from their ancestors. Several thousand years of selection have transformed the eggplant from a bitter-fruited plant in India, to a small, white, egg-shaped fruit, to the giant purple variety now commonly consumed in America. Eggplant is perennial but not frost hardy and requires greenhouse shelter to overwinter successfully.

Though it is common to assume eggplant is only purple, like tomato is only red, this is not the case with either. There are red, orange, pink, white, yellow, light green, purple, and purple and white-striped varieties. The tomato-fruited eggplants are bitterer and soft inside while other eggplants are solid, harder fruits.

Inbreeding, perfect flowered, and self-compatible, eggplants are most commonly self-pollinated. Isolation of just 50 feet is acceptable to maintain the purity of the eggplant seed, which is harvested when the plant is fully ripe, well after it is edible.

The color of the plant will dull and the fruit will harden further, indicating the seeds are mature. Seeds harvested too early will not grow.

Similar to other Solanaceae, it is best to pulverize the flesh of the eggplant using a coarse grater to harvest its seeds. Soak the eggplant in water, and agitate it. The flesh will float to the top, and the seeds will fall to the bottom. This is another task well suited for young gardeners in the family. Lay the seeds out for several days to dry, and then package them for storage. Limit exposure of these seeds to heat, humidity, and light until you intend to sow them.

Tomatillo

These little tomato-like green fruits are harder than tomatoes and grow inside a papery husk. They are very commonly used in Mexican cuisine and widely used within the Southwest United States. They make excellent container plants and will grow well with the support of a tomato cage. Gardeners with limited ground space can appreciate this plant's vertical growing habit.

Tomatillos are inbreeding, perfect, and self-pollinating. They are perennial plants that are often grown as annuals because they often do not thrive in subsequent growing seasons as well as in the first season. They are also easier to grow from seed than to care for over the winter. The seeds are as easy to harvest as the tomato's seed. Put the whole fruit in the blender or food processor, turn it on, and extract the seeds similar to any other Solanaceae. And like other Solanaceae, lay the seeds out for several days to dry and then package them for storage. Limit their exposure to heat, humidity, and light until you intend to sow them.

Chinese lantern

Chinese lantern is closely related to the tomatillo, but differs in that it has smaller fruits that are encased in vibrant orange or red, heart-shaped husks. It can also be grown in regions that tomatillo cannot and vice versa. They grow as annuals in colder climates that tomatillo will not survive in. The unripe fruits are toxic, and care should be taken to not allow children or pets to eat them before they are ripe.

Chinese lantern is pollinated and harvested for seed in much the same manner as tomatillo. They are inbreeding, perfect, and self-pollinating. They survive into subsequent growing seasons as they are hardier than the tomatillo and have a strong growing habit. They can be quite invasive in the garden and may require pruning. Just like the tomato, blending the whole fruit will loosen the seed so you can easily separate them to dry and store. Lay the seeds out for several days to dry, and then package them for storage. Keep the seeds from heat, humidity, and light to prevent their decay.

Cubitaceae Family

Cucurbits are a wonderful, large family of garden fruit that grow along broad-leaved, tendril-bearing vines that mound and fill the garden until fall. The majority of cucurbits are grown as annuals, though there are a few perennials in the family. What makes this family unique is that the fruits are used for food and function, with archaeological discoveries of gourd dishes used several thousand years ago. The family is also monoecious, which means it produces flowers that are singularly male or female, on a single plant.

TABLE 10: COMMON SPECIES OF THE CUBITACEAE FAMILY, BY GENUS

Citrullus	
Lanatus	watermelon
Cucumis	
Anguria	West Indian gherkin or burr cucumber
Melo	muskmelon, cantaloupe, honeydew, sugar melon
Metuliferus	Kiwano or African horned cucumber
Sativus	garden cucumber
Cucurbita	
Ficifolia	fig leaf gourd
Foetidissima	Missouri gourda, buffalo gourd, calabazilla
Maxima	winter squash
Mixta	pumpkin
Moschata	crookneck squash, tropical pumpkin
Pepo	field pumpkin
Lagenaria	
Siceraria	bottle gourd
Luffa	
Acutangula	angled luffa
Aegyptiaca	smooth luffa, sponge gourd
Momordica	
Balsamina	balsam apple
Charantia	balsam pear, bitter melon
Sechium	
Edule	chayote, or vegetable pear
Sicana	
Odorifera	cassabanana
Trichosanthes	
Anguina	serpent gourd

Isolation and pollination notes: Because cucurbits are monoecious, they require insects to pollinate and fertilize. Of course, this means they are easily cross-pollinated and varieties of the same species (e.g. maxima or mixta) can cross with each other. If you are only growing one type of each species, your concern will be with making sure your garden is sufficiently isolated from surrounding plants, and the bees will do the pollinating for you. Isolation distances of less than 100 feet have been shown to effectively contain cross-pollination. However, if you are not isolated, hand pollination works well thanks to the large, singular blooms.

To hand pollinate cucurbits, first you must know which flower is pistillate and which is staminate. The male, or staminate, flowers have a consistent stalk right up to the flower base. Female flowers, or pistillate flowers, widen (sometimes considerably) before the base of the flower. This widening is the unfertilized ovary of the plant. In either case, to prevent contamination, before the flowers bloom and the petals open, tape them shut.

All but one variety — the hard-shelled gourd — open in the morning. The hard-shelled gourd opens in the night and requires taping in the morning. As the plants begin flowering, observe that some will appear green and not ready to open, others will seem to be almost ready, and still others will be in bloom. A key indicator that a flower is ready to open is that the seams between the petals will change color and the tips of the flower will begin to curl open. Taping those that you suspect will open the next morning on the prior evening will prevent contamination, and you can locate and hand pollinate them in the morning. Placing masking tape around the top of the flower petals provides a barrier between your flower and its pollinators. Immediate pollination will make sure you have the most viable pollen and eggs to work with.

To pollinate, locate a male flower and remove the tape. Gently remove the petals, exposing the anthers. Keep the bees off of it at all times to avoid contamination.

Open a female, locate its stigma, rub the anthers against them, and then close the female. It is important to reclose the female to ensure it is not later contaminated by undesired pollen, either from insects or other unintentional pollinator. You should fertilize each female several times with different males to ensure successful pollination. Males may be used on more than one female as well. Whatever process you decide, make sure the flowers are not contaminated, or they will be worthless to save seeds from. (They will still make good fruit though.)

Cucurbits are limited in their ability to produce fruits. They will continue to flower even after the last fruits set, and later blooms will not form fruit. If you are hand pollinating, you should wait to hand pollinate until after the first couple flowers set to fruit. As soon as you begin to notice their ovaries enlarging, remove the early fruit and hand pollinate new flowers. The energy the plant was putting in to the first fruits will divert into the ones you have hand pollinated.

Harvesting seed: The fruits of the cucurbit must reach full maturity before you can harvest them for seed. The seeds are best when the ripe fruit is picked from the vine and then harvested about 20 days after picking. This results in the highest number of available and mature seeds. Seeds are scraped from the inside of the ripened fruits and then rinsed before drying.

Fermentation helps both clean the new seeds and prepare them for germination. You can begin the fermentation process by soaking the seeds and their coatings in water at a ratio of one-part seed to one-part water and setting the container aside in a warm place. Fermentation causes an unpleasant odor, so it is best left out of popular areas in your home. Leave the mixture for up to three days, making sure to stir it a couple times a day to keep fermentation consistent. It will likely mold over while the process is advancing. The extra pulps and seed casings, as well as nonviable seeds, will float to the surface. Pour off the waste, and rinse the seeds that remain. They are then ready to dry and store, as with most seeds, in a dark, dry, cool area.

If you would rather skip the fermentation, you can for all cucurbits except cucumbers because they require fermentation. Studies show that germination rates of all Cucurbitaceae family members increase when fermented, so if your goal is production, it is best to allow the plant to ferment. If you do decide to bypass the fermentation process, pick the seeds from the ripened fruits by hand, and allow them to dry before storing as you would store fermented seeds.

Watermelon

The watermelon is America's largest edible fruit. When ripe, the sweet juicy pulp is eaten raw, and its seeds may be roasted as a snack. Watermelons can range in size from about 5 to 50 pounds, depending upon the cultivar, climate, and care they receive.

Some growers in the central southern United States achieve fruits in excess of 100 pounds, but the trend is for icebox size melons of 8 to 12 pounds. Triploid or seedless watermelons are increasing in popularity as well.

Watermelon is a monoecious annual. The stems or runners may extend up to about 15 feet and are covered in wide leaves. The fruit varies according to the variety: oblong to round; light green to dark green or mottled rinds; red, yellow, light green, or white flesh; and white, yellow, brown, black, or reddish black seeds. It is a warm-season crop, and fruit matures best at higher daytime temperatures with warm nights. Like other cucurbits, there is a limit to each plant's production, and the watermelon produces one to two good melons per plant with seedless varieties producing slightly more.

Staminate flowers outnumber pistillate flowers on the watermelon plant by about a six to one ratio, and you will need to tape back six male flowers at night and pluck them in the morning to pollinate each female flower. The flowers open just hours after sunrise. Although most pollination takes place before noon, the stigma is receptive throughout the day. Taping the pollinated females closed prevents unintended pollination, as insects naturally pollinate them.

It is easiest to determine if a watermelon is ripe by checking the indentation opposite the stem. The melon is ripe and ready for harvest when that indentation becomes dry and brown. Remove the seeds from the flesh after waiting 20 days, and ferment them. Then, they are ready to dry and preserve. Set them in a warm place to dry, and then as soon as they are thoroughly dry, place them in storage in a dark, dry, cool place.

Muskmelon, cantaloupe, honeydew, casaba, snake melon or Armenian cucumber, Asian pickling melon, pocket melon, mango melon

Cucumis melo has oval or kidney shaped leaves with between five and seven lobes. Plants produce trailing vines and yellow flowers much like cucumbers, but *cucumis melo* flowers may be male, female, or perfect. The three botanical varieties within the species can and do cross-pollinate freely. The muskmelon, *reticulous*, has orange flesh and a netted rind, often wrongly called cantaloupe. This is what is typically found in grocery stores. However, the true cantaloupe, *cantaloupensis*, is in the same family but not grown in the United States. It is similar to the muskmelon but has a harder, rougher rind. The winter melons, *inodorus*, include casaba, Crenshaw, honeydew, Christmas, and Persian melon. These ripen later in the growing season. Muskmelon is a popular fruit that is eaten fresh or can be jarred or frozen.

Melons have a long growing season that ranges from 90 to 125 days of moderate to warm temperatures. They are outbreeders and bear particular difficulties. Though they are easy to pollinate by insects, the flowers are generally quite small and more time-consuming to pollinate by hand. These plants also like to perfect their own fruit and will abort about eight of every ten fruits they produce. So, between taking longer to pollinate and a large ratio of fruit failure, melons can be very discouraging to grow from seed. Gardeners with more time and patience will succeed. Some keys to success are pollinating as soon as the morning dew is dry, using the very first female flower to open on each plant as it is the most likely to succeed, and be persistent. Once harvest time comes, and you have fresh fruit to enjoy and viable seeds to save (in the same manner as the watermelon), it will be a sweet reward for your dedication.

Cucumbers

Cucumber varieties grown in home gardens include the crisp slicer or fresh salad varieties, pickling varieties (which can also be used fresh), dwarf-vined varieties, and bush varieties. Breeders are engineering new hybridizations of cucumber, advertising them as all-female, or **gynoecious**. On a normal cucumber plant, the first ten to 20 flowers are male, and for every female flower, which are the only flowers that produce fruit, another ten to 20 male flowers emerge on the vine. So, plant breeders select and breed female flower-laden vines, isolating that quality so that growers can produce more fruits. Some of the new varieties have only female flowers and others have a more even ratio of female to male flowers. There are also bush varieties of cucumber available from seed from commercial growers. These varieties generally produce well in limited space and may be a desirable alternative in a small garden. They will also do well on a patio garden in containers.

Cucumbers are daylight sensitive, and the best yield of female flowers comes on days when the sunlight averages 11 hours. They are outbreeders, as with the rest of the family, and require isolation in conjunction with taping and hand pollination to produce the best seed yields.

Cucumbers are ripe for picking when they begin to soften a little and the color begins to change. The hundreds of seeds that each cucumber produces require fermentation for successful germination. The process, described in detail in the Cucurbitaceae family "Seed Harvesting" section, requires removing the seeds and soaking them in a water bath in a warm place for several days before rinsing them for drying.

The squashes of the Cucurbitaceae family

Squash is one of the most fascinating-looking fruits grown in the garden. All shapes and sizes abound in the multiple subspecies of Cucurbitaceae that comprise the squash varieties. Wrinkled, warted, horned, knobby, in yellows, greens, oranges, stripes — squash is without a doubt a plant entertaining to the eye. Squash exists in many varieties, and those varieties belong to six different species. When planting squash and planning to harvest seed from it, pay attention to the species you plant. Any two varieties in the same species can, and likely will, cross each other. If you plant one variety of each of the six species available, you will not have to worry about unwanted cross-pollination. Otherwise, you should plan to isolate (preferably by taping) and hand pollinate the varieties you intend to harvest seed from.

If there are adequate pollinators (for example, plenty of bees) in the garden, then open pollination is an easy choice for squashes. The flowers are very attractive to insects and will not need any additional help in pollinating to get a good fruit set. Of course, if you grow more than one variety of the same species of squash, or if you want to choose the healthiest specimens to cross-pollinate, you will be isolating and hand pollinating to get healthy, viable seeds from your squashes.

The squash's flowers open early in the morning so that they have the most opportunity for pollination. This is one reason it is good to keep photos and a journal of your garden's characteristics. With photos, you can see what your plants look like right before the flowers open, which is important to know in the case of squash. It is not useful the first year necessarily, but you will know what to expect in subsequent years. With squash, you must be able to distinguish between male and female flowers. Staminate squash flowers grow on long stems. They mature and are fertile before female flowers on the same plant. Pistillate flowers appear to have miniature squash at the base of the flower. They usually have shorter stems as well.

To hand pollinate squash, select the male and female flowers you wish to pollinate before they open. You should tape them shut the day prior to them opening so they are not naturally contaminated. The next morning, collect the male flowers by removing them from the plant. Remove the petals to expose the anthers, which contain the pollen. Rub the anthers on the female stigmas to transfer the pollen. Use a few male flowers for each female to ensure good pollination. Then tape the petals of the female flower back shut. You can put a little tuft of cotton inside the flower before you tape it shut. This helps keep insects out and lowers the flower's risk of contamination. Label pollinated flowers so that you can easily find and save their seed. You could label them with surveyor's tape around the stem or use little pipe cleaners from craft stores, as they are gentle and removable.

Allow the squash to ripen fully on the plant before removing it to harvest the seeds. Dig the seeds out of the squash and set them on a cookie sheet or stone to dry. They can be a little sticky on paper. Once they are dry, store squash seeds in a cool, dark place.

Hard-shelled gourd

The hard shell of the gourd is significant in society. Archaeologists have uncovered bowls, cups, tools, ladles, and all sorts of useful items early-civilized cultures in America made from gourds. They are not routinely grown for their fruit, and because most of the applications for their hard shells have been replaced — bowls are now ceramic, ladles are metal — they are not as widely desired or grown. Nonetheless, they deserve a place in the garden, as they can be consumed when young, and there are many applications, though not as popular. Gourds make excellent décor and artwork, and they are still wonderful rattles (once the toxins are leeched from their rind).

Horticulturists recommend ¼ to ½ mile isolation for gourds. These plants are the odd ones in the family as the flowers open in the evening and have to be taped in the morning. Hand pollination should take place at night, and this provides one way to space out some of your garden tasks.

Harvest the gourd when it is ripe, and allow it to dry entirely with the seeds inside. They will rattle when they are dry. The seeds can be removed through any opening in the hardened shell, so plan your gourd use around the harvest. Store your seeds in a cool, dark location until you are ready to plant them. Preserve the shell in the form you will use it, and harvest seeds to grow more beautiful gourds the next year.

> **One note about gourds:** Have fun with them. Cross them on purpose, and isolate the crosses in a cage so they do not pollinate your pure ones. Crossed gourd seeds can produce some lovely shells.

Angled luffa and smooth luffa

Is it food or a tool? It is both. Though the immature fruits of the luffa plant make for delicious culinary treats in Asian and Oriental cuisine, it is often harvested, and the porous flesh is used as an exfoliating sponge. Luffa shares many characteristics with its cucurbit family. It is an annual, outbreeding, insect-pollinated, heat-loving plant. It requires isolation (preferably by taping the individual flowers) so that the seeds are pure and not hybrid, remaining viable. It is harvested like the gourd, with the seed remaining in its shell to dry. Once the seeds are dry, store them in a cool, dark location.

Chayote or vegetable pear

Chayote is a tropical region plant and perennial, unlike most of the cucurbits. Its tuberous roots survive frosts and cool temperatures above freezing. If started indoors and dug up for overwintering, chayote makes a cooler region perennial as well. There are several varieties of the plant, but only one is available in the United States from commercial growers. Because of this, isolation is unnecessary in most cases, and you can enjoy the produce of the chayote with little fuss. This includes early shoots eaten like asparagus, edible roots that can be prepared like potatoes, and fruits that can be used in a range of foods.

Allow the chayote to ripen fully on the plant before removing it to harvest the seeds. Dig the seeds out of the fruit, and set them on a cookie sheet or stone to dry. They can be a little sticky on paper. Once dry, store chayote seeds in a cool dark place.

Vitaceae Family

Grapes are practically the only well-known member of the Vitaceae family, but what a significant family member they are. The Vitaceae family is a large, diverse, and seemingly disjointed collection of plant species and cultivars, which includes Virginia creeper, a type of prolific ivy-like vine, but no other significant fruit varieties.

Grapes

When thinking about the possibility of growing grapes, do not discount the idea of having them as part of your small garden setting merely because you might think that they require a large growing space. Grapes are customarily grown in vineyards, but a vine or two can just as easily be cultivated in your own small garden. You can even grow grapes in a large container as long as there is enough room for the root growth that a grapevine will eventually produce.

Because the maturing fruit and foliage of the vines will become heavy, the vines will need support after they have reached a certain level of maturity. You can provide support by any number of methods, like trellises and arbors, which are discussed in Chapter 13. The method of training a fruit or flowering tree onto a flattened trellis is called espalier and has been used for centuries by horticulturists who were faced with space limitations. It is an effective way to grow small species of fruit trees in even the most modest of gardens. While espalier might look difficult to achieve, it is the same mechanism used to support grapevines grown on trellises. Once you have completed your grapevine training project, it might strike you that the technique that you used for the grapes could also be adapted to accommodate larger fruits, such as plums and peaches, for instance.

There are many grape varieties, and personal choice plays a role in selecting which type you choose to plant. Concord grapes, for example, are an old-fashioned variety that offers delicious fruit and prodigious yield. They are commonly used in jams. No matter which variety you choose to plant, the seeds from the grapes that are not eaten can be easily extracted either by hand or by putting them in a blender.

To remove seeds from grapes by hand:

1. Cut each grape into half.

2. Using the tip of a small spoon or butter knife, carefully dig out the individual seeds.

3. Carefully separate the flesh from the seeds, and rinse the seeds in a sieve or other strainer, making sure that the holes in the strainer are not big enough to allow the seeds to slip through.

4. Dry the seeds by laying them out in a warm place for several days. Because the seeds are larger, they will require more time to dry than many other seeds. Ensure you do not put them in direct sunlight, as that will cause the seeds to burn.

5. After drying, store in an airtight and watertight container in a cool place.

Though the seeds are easy to extract, dry, and store, most grapes are propagated from cuttings, rather than grown from seeds. Growing grapes from cuttings ensures the offspring carry the same traits as its parent plant. Grapes grown from seed carry any combination of the genes of the parent plants. So, vines that produce well, bear delicious fruit, produce good quantities, and have good health can turn into many more vines that all have the characteristics of the parent plant. This is especially essential to vintners who rely on the consistency of their produce's qualities to make quality wines.

As far as using grape seeds is concerned, initially gardeners propagated early varieties of grapes from wild seedlings that they found desirable. These plants were simply the inadvertent result of accidental crosses between vines. As plant knowledge increased, so did gardeners' decision to actively propagate the plants to control pollination. Gardeners carefully chose which varieties served as the parents for their seed production endeavors, sort of like arranged marriages.

Depending on the individual vine, flowers might be female, male, or perfect. The overwhelming majority of cultivated varieties are perfect. Vines with perfect flowers are generally preferred because they are self-fruitful, and they are particularly desired where space is of the essence because every vine planted can bear fruit. In both staminate and perfect flowers, the pollen is shed by the wind and carried up to 20 feet. When the pollen lands on the stigma of a female or perfect flower, it begins the fertilization process. Though it can travel up to 20 feet, pollen need only travel millimeters to the stigma of the same perfect flower on a self-fruitful vine.

As with most hand-pollinating endeavors, isolation from insects is necessary. Though bees are not significant pollinators, insects can inadvertently cross-pollinate grapes. It is a rare occurrence, but important to isolate for guaranteed seed purity. The wind certainly is a significant pollinator, so isolation distances are critical for vines. Hand pollination has greater value for home gardeners because the products of the seeds they will collect will be long-standing members of their gardens. To cross-pollinate grapes, identify and collect or isolate the pollen sources and potential ovaries, rub the pollen parts against the receptive parts, and isolate them until the fruit is set.

If the male variety you choose to pollinate the female with is fertile significantly earlier than the female, collect and store the pollen. Collect pollen by drying the anthers for a couple of days. Shake the pollen over a mirror then scrape it into a labeled vial with a razor blade. You can store the dried pollen at 0 degrees in a deep freezer. It will maintain its viability for some time, but once it has dried and aged, it will never be as viable as fresh pollen. Some pollen lasts longer than other pollen, but in home storage, you should not expect it to last beyond the current growing season. To use the pollen, thaw it in its sealed vial until it reaches room temperature to keep it from building condensation inside. Do this right before the female is receptive, and discard remaining pollen, as freezing it several times will decrease its viability. If you have multiple plants on which you want to use pollen from one male, store the pollen in multiple vials, thawing only what you need as you go. Using stored pollen is the only means of fertilizing a female flower that becomes receptive before the male bears pollen (assuming the flowers are not perfect). In perfect flowers, it does not matter which parent is the male or female because the cross will be the same, so you may collect the pollen from the earlier breeding plant to use on the later breeding one.

To understand the kind of undertaking this is, you must know that the flowers on grapevines grow in clusters containing dozens to hundreds of individual, tiny flowers. Preparing them requires a set of tweezers and a lot of time and patience. Every flower must be pollinated on the clusters you intend to harvest for seed so they are not inadvertently pollinated by a later source and contaminated. You also want the highest yield possible in order to reap the most seeds from your painstaking labor or love.

The most important goal in preparing female flowers is to prevent accidental pollination before you can apply the chosen male's pollen. Before the flower opens, it is covered by a membrane known as a **calyptra**. This "cap" naturally dries and comes off on its own when the flower is ready for pollination. In a perfect flower, though, it must be removed along with the unripe anthers a day or two before the stigma is receptive to prevent self-pollination. This can be done before the cap is completely dry. This process is called **emasculation.**

Once you have emasculated perfect flowers, or a few days before pistillate flowers are receptive, you will want to bag the entire cluster in a nonporous bag to keep the wind-borne pollen from reaching the stigma. Generally, a bead of moisture on the stigma indicates the flower is ready to receive the pollen. Dip a sterile soft brush in the pollen, and brush every stigma of every female flower gently but thoroughly. Reapply the bag to the cluster to prevent further fertilization and protect the fruit from hazards like birds and bugs. The berries will mature and ripen successfully inside its bag.

At harvest time, collect the clusters, extract the single seeds from within their berries, and drop them in a bowl of water. Like most seeds, viable grape seeds will sink, and the bad ones will float. Lay the good seeds out to dry on a paper towel before storing them in a cool, dark, dry place.

Fruit Trees

Because the results from cross-pollinating apples and pears can be so unpredictable, growing these two particular types of fruit from seed can be problematic. To avoid any unexpected surprises in the quality of the resulting fruit, they are usually propagated by grafting cuttings or buds onto prepared rootstocks, which are transplanted after having matured into seedlings. **Rootstocks** are trees that are grown specifically for their root portions to graft cuttings onto. Trees that have good, strong rooting characteristics are commonly used for rootstock, while those that produce quality fruit are used to graft. These become clones of the parent fruit-producing tree. **Grafting** is artificially attaching a cut portion of a plant onto a parent of the same species. Successful grafting is an art; it is exacting and unforgiving. Prepared rootstocks also can be quite expensive ($25 to $35), and there is no guarantee your grafting will take. The cost issues alone could prevent you from even attempting to grow such fruit trees, and the difficulty of performing a successful graft with all its variables further complicates the process for the home gardener.

There are varieties of fruit trees, mostly those that produce peaches, nectarines, and apricots, that can be grown very successfully from their own seeds, and can be grown in practically every portion of North America. In fact, peach trees — the seeds of which originally thought to have been brought here from China — are found on both the East and West coasts, and everywhere in between. Peaches, nectarines, and apricots are easy to grow from seed, and the trees produced from such seed will bear fruit by the third year after they are planted. It is best to obtain seeds from trees that grow locally because you can be familiar with how the fruit tastes before you grow it. Choosing a local variety of fruit tree will also give you confidence that the trees will flourish in the climate and soil available in your garden. Try the peaches and nectarines from the farmers markets and produce stands in your area that you know sell locally grown products, and then save the seeds from the fruit that is superior. It is important to use locally grown produce, rather than something grown off-season in another part of the country, as you may not be able to grow that variety of fruit in your region and within your growing season.

Once you have chosen the fruit that you want to use, enjoy it by eating the fruit raw or using in baking or other recipes. Remove the pits, and place them out of the way to dry for a few days. They need to be as dry as possible, as this makes them easier to pry open. After the outside shells are dried, you can crack them open and remove the little inside kernel, which is the actual seed. If you have difficulty opening the pits, you may use a hammer or even a conventional nutcracker to assist the process. Remove the seeds and store them in an airtight container in the refrigerator or some other place where they will be kept cool until you are ready to use them. If needed, before storing, dry the seeds further in a warm place out of direct sunlight.

Pollination and How it Affects Production

Once they have matured enough to flower, your fruit trees are ready to pollinate and, hopefully, bear fruit. There are almost as many ways for trees to pollinate and be pollinated, as there are types of trees. Without pollination, the trees can be filled with fragrant, beautiful pink and white blooms, but if the blooms are not pollinated, they will simply drop off the tree, and no fruit will replace them. Pollination is necessary in order for trees to produce the seed that will eventually cause fruit to form.

Many fruit trees are self-pollinating, and then there are those that have to be pollinated through an outside means, usually biotic. You can take specific steps to increase the chances that the trees will be pollinated by an outside source. One way you can do this is to encourage bees in the garden. By planting certain types of flowers — bee balm, Black-eyed Susan, coneflowers — you will attract more bees into the area, increasing the opportunities for insect pollination. Try not to use insecticides until after pollination, if at all. Chemicals are harmful to bees and the blooms, as well as other insects that can actually help pollination. They are also suspected carcinogens in many cases and have unknown long-term health implications. You can also encourage cross-pollination by planting more than one variety of the same type of tree (or acceptable crosses) in close proximity, which will help even self-pollinating trees.

If all else fails, pollinate your own trees by hand. If you are not seeing bees in the garden for whatever reason, you can break off a flowering branch of one tree and wave it among the flowers of another tree. The pollen that is emitted will fall onto the flowers of the other tree, thereby pollinating most, if not all, of the flowers.

When your fruit trees have started to produce fruit, and you become familiar with what the usual yield of each tree is, you might need to thin your crop. **Thinning** is the process of removing a certain number of plants, or in this case fruits, so that the sturdier, healthier specimens have a better chance of survival. If you are the type of gardener who agonizes over thinning out carrots and onions, it may be even more difficult to pick fruit off a tree before it has become fully ripened. In some cases, thinning must be done if you want the fruit coming from the tree in question to be of proper size. If the fruit a certain tree produces is undersized when fully ripe, this could be because there is too much fruit on the tree altogether. The tree is expending energy to produce fruit, so, in order to get the biggest specimens possible, some thinning must be done. It is best to do this when the fruit is still small, as early in the season as possible. Depending on the zone of the country, this could be as early as March or April. If the fruit is not thinned out, the tree will produce a crop of small, immature specimens as compared to a crop of full-sized acceptable fruits. Fruit should be thinned evenly over the whole tree. Look for fruits that appear smaller, irregular, or have infestation to remove first.

Peach, nectarine, sour cherry, almond, plum, and apricot

Apricot, peach, nectarine, almond, plum, and sour cherry comprise the Prunus family. The **deciduous** varieties of the family (those that lose their leaves in the cold season) need to be grown in temperate climates, whereas the evergreen members of the family can survive cooler temperatures. Nearly all of the common varieties of Prunus are self-compatible and do not require insect cross-pollination. However, insect presence does aid in self-pollination, and bees should be encouraged to help the blooms get maximum amounts of pollination. A few varieties of these fruit trees are self-incompatible. You will want to ensure that you have a compatible second variety and plentiful pollinators to cross them if you desire growing one of the self-incompatible varieties. Make sure you ask your supplier if the tree you are purchasing is self-compatible or if it requires a cross-pollinating companion in the garden. Isolation of a self-compatible tree or a set of companion pollinating trees by 50 feet is sufficient to limit cross-pollination. Preserve these seeds in the same manner as others. Remove the seed from the flesh, allow it to dry thoroughly, and place it in cool, dry storage in a dark place.

Sweet cherry

Sweet cherry is one of the Prunus family varieties that is often self-incompatible. Only a handful of sweet cherry varieties are self-fruitful, and the rest require a cross-pollinator. If you plan to grow sweet cherry, plan to purchase two varieties (at least) if you want them to bear fruit. Adding to the complexity, many varieties will not cross-pollinate each other. Double check with your supplier to make sure you are getting varieties that will work together. In the following chart are some common varieties of sweet cherry. Isolation of 50 feet is sufficient to keep unintentional pollinators from crossing sweet cherry varieties you do not want crossed. *Check the Appendix for a chart detailing which varieties of sweet cherry should and should not be pollinated.*

To preserve the seeds, remove and dry the pits. Then store them in a cool place that has low humidity and preferably is dark. This prevents rapid decay of the nutrient store of the seed.

Apple

In order for apple to set fruit, it must be cross-pollinated. Each variety of apple tree should be cross-pollinated with a different variety of apple or with a crabapple variety. Although some varieties, like the Jonathan, Gala, and Granny Smith, are considered self-fruitful, it is merely an anatomical possibility. These varieties will set more fruit with more seeds and better size every year that they are cross-pollinated. Some other apple varieties, including Winesap and Jonagold, produce sterile pollen and cannot be used to pollinate other apple varieties.

To achieve the best fruit set on your apple trees, you must pollinate the **king blossom**, which is the largest and first flower to open (similar to the queen blossom in cucurbits) in the flower cluster. To do so, the pollination dates of the varieties you plan to cross must overlap. Plan your tree plantings so that the trees that are closest to each other are the ones whose pollination overlaps. The maximum separation distance between semi-dwarf apple varieties is 50 feet. If you plant them further apart, you significantly decrease the ability of pollinators to cross them, and you will get very little fruit. At 50 feet or less, bees can successfully carry pollen from blooms on one tree to blooms on the next. For dwarf varieties, the distance is even less — 20 feet.

Manchurian crabapple is often used to pollinate early and mid-blooming apple trees, and Snowdrift crabapple is used for mid- and late-blooming apple trees. When using a crabapple tree as a pollinator, the tree must be planted within close proximity to the tree(s) it will be pollinating. *Check the Appendix for charts on which varieties of apples you should cross-breed, as well as which times during the season it is best to pollinate the fruits.*

In a small garden setting where you may only have room for one apple tree, you can introduce branches of open fresh blossoms from another apple tree or crabapple tree as a pollinator, placing them in buckets of water that are hung in the tree. That is a temporary solution that can be done from year to year, but a permanent solution to ensure pollination where only a single tree is planted is to graft a pollinating apple variety onto the existing tree. This is a complicated process that requires much attention, as essentially you are connecting raw tissues of two plants together in the hopes they will fuse. Disease, rot, and scar tissue are some of the potential side effects.

Apple seeds are very apparent in the fruit. Simply cut open the fruit, and remove the seeds from its center. Dry the seeds thoroughly by allowing them to sit out in a warm location, and then store them in a cool, dry, and dark area.

Pear

The majority of pear varieties are self-incompatible. Despite that fact, nearly all pears make suitable pollinators for each other as long as they bloom at the same time. However, there are a few exceptions. Seckel is not a good pollinator for delicious Bartlett. Even though the Anjou, Bartlett, and Kieffer pears are partially self-fertile, they should still be cross-pollinated. This will ensure that the fruit set is plentiful and healthy on the trees. Pear flowers do not produce a large quantity of nectar, so the bees that are nearby are not as attracted to them. Two ways to combat this shortage of pollinators is to introduce additional bees (you can rent hives from bee farmers during growing season) and to eliminate detractors like dandelions and other flowers that will easily lure the bees away with the promise of an easier supply of nectar.

Like most fruit trees, pear pollen does not carry very well on insects, so minimal isolation is needed to keep undesired cross-pollination from occurring. Twenty-five to 50 feet is sufficient between flowering trees to prevent them from crossing. Remove the seed from the ripened fruit, dry it, and put it in the refrigerator in a jar with some silica salt to store it.

Plum

There are two general categories of plums to consider when addressing pollination: European, or prune-type, and Japanese. Most of the European plums either require or will benefit from cross-pollination. The pollinating plant must be from another European variety, as they are otherwise incompatible. There are a few European plums, like the Stanley and Damson plums, that are self-fertile. The Japanese plums require pollination from another Japanese plum or an American-Japanese hybrid to ensure successful fruit set. You will not need more than 50 feet of isolation with plums to prevent unintended cross-pollination.

Remove the seed from the ripened fruit, dry it, and store it in the refrigerator in a jar with some silica salt. These seeds are typically quite large and so cannot be stored in envelopes like most small seeds.

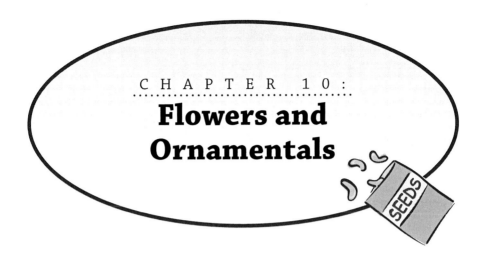

CHAPTER 10:
Flowers and Ornamentals

To those who garden, one of the reasons to garden is because the gorgeous world around us could not exist without flowers. To imagine the world without flowers is to imagine a drab, colorless place. Flowers can be found in every form of art and have been a part of the lives of human beings since prehistoric times. Ancient graves, unearthed in caves in the Middle East, uncovered skeletons that had been buried with flowers alongside them. Ever since those primitive times, humans have used flowers in symbolic ways to commemorate important events in their lives, from the romantic to the funereal.

According to scientists, there are more than 275,000 species of flowering plants. Flowers exist in every place on earth that can sustain plant life. The many categories of flowers that cover the planet provide an almost limitless selection from which to choose. Whereas gardeners used to be constrained by geographical restrictions, now if you want to grow a particular species of flower, all you have to do is find a reliable source and obtain a seed, bulb, or plant to grow an exotic specimen in your own house or garden. In this way, unique and unusual flowers have traveled from faraway places and made their way into our lives. You may not have grown up on acre-plus gardens, or even had a simple plot at home, but that does not mean you cannot start growing flowers now in whatever space you have available. Growing flowers is a labor of love dedicated to pure aesthetic pleasure. That pleasure is rooted in good design, planning your layout and workload, and making sure the framework is in place for enjoying your time gardening.

Planning Your Flower Garden

The flowers that will be discussed in this chapter, and the seed saving methods used for each type of flower are some of the most popular and commonly used by gardeners across the country. You can use this information to plant a flower garden from which you can collect your own seed and regenerate for years to come.

While the majority of these flowers will fall into the biennial and perennial categories, seed saving and preservation techniques for some annuals will also be included here. Perennials are the garden's stability — the backbone of the garden. They are the plants the gardener relies on to return each year, and the structure around which the rest of the garden takes shape. They emerge in the same place and provide the comfort and familiarity of a garden's design. Even though they return each year, perennials also fall victim to the same effects of aging as any other living organism. Because they eventually die, either from age, disease, climate extreme, or pestilence, it is necessary to ensure you have seed from which to grow future generations. If you are interested in crossbreeding perennials, their pollination habits and knowledge of how to collect their seed is crucial.

Biennials and annuals are also very useful in the flower garden. While perennials are the basic structure of the garden, biennials and annuals serve to fill in the flower beds around those perennials. They also provide the changes each year in color and texture and allow the gardener to experiment and make inexpensive changes to fulfill desires or suit current trends. Biennials and annuals tend to be less expensive, more varied in color and size, and readily available in garden centers when they are in season. Seed can be collected from biennials and annuals to make yearly plantings more cost effective.

Like fruits and vegetables, the seeds from flowers of all types have a limited shelf life. For most, you can expect up to three years of viability at a 50 percent rate of germination. This means most plants will provide you with seeds that (at least) half of which will grow when planted within three years of saving. Many have longer viability, but three years is a good rule of thumb unless you have advanced preservation means like **cryogenics** (extreme low temperature preservation usually only attainable in a lab setting). Some flower species that do not produce seeds will not last as long, so that annual collection will be required to ensure you have viable seed stock.

TABLE 14 APPROXIMATE LONGEVITY (IN YEARS) OF SELECTED FLOWER SEEDS
Adapted from Bienz, D.R. 1980. *The why and how of home horticulture.* W.H. Freeman and Company, New York.

Longevity	Flower Varieties
5	carnation, chrysanthemum, hollyhock, nasturtium, salpiglossis, sweet sultans, zinnia
4	sweet alyssum
3	African daisy, cosmos, dusty miller, marigold, pansy, petunia, scabiosa, shasta daisy, snapdragon, verbena
2	aster, phlox, sweet pea
1	delphinium, columbine

Saving flower seeds is a mostly straightforward, somewhat intuitive process, and there are some basic considerations to remember. The gardener should pay attention and become acquainted with the development patterns of the seeds they sowed. Careful garden journaling and acute observation are important for determining when the plant will need which care. For maximum viability, a plant's seeds must be harvested at just the right time. The gardener seeking to harvest seeds should observe the plant's seed heads or pods routinely as they develop. On most flowers, the pods will indicate they are ready to harvest by becoming dry and brittle. Look to the sweet pea as a good example. The seeds of the sweet pea will be green if you harvest them too soon. The green seeds are not fully developed, will not dry properly, and will likely not be viable when it comes time to plant them. Conversely, if you wait too long, the dried pods will scatter their seeds. It is best to observe and note the patterns in your journal, so you have the harvesting information to reference the next year.

When going out to harvest seeds, take along the tools you will need. Bring gloves, garden shears, and something to collect the seeds in. For seed heads, which are generally larger than most individual seeds, paper lunch sacks or even grocery sacks will work. If you are just shaking the seeds from some flower heads, bring a handful of snack or sandwich-sized bags that are perfect for small amounts of seed.

Choose the ripe seed heads that are dry. Many will rattle and the pods will start to split when you squeeze them. Many seeds produced in seed heads and pods will rattle when they are ready (columbine is one that comes to mind). Most seed heads and pods are ready to harvest when they readily snap off their stems. If they bend, give them more time unless the seeds are prone to shattering, in which case you will want to harvest the seed heads just before the stems are completely dry.

Attempting to harvest seeds when they are wet can be an exercise in futility. They will stick to the plant, your fingers, and anywhere you do not want them to. Either wait for drier weather, or pick the seed heads to dry out where they are sheltered from humidity.

Seeds should be dried in a warm and well-ventilated room. The optimal temperature to dry most seeds at is about 90 degrees, but do not let drying temperatures exceed 100 degrees, as it will damage the seeds. Drying seeds in the direct, hot sun will damage them as well. You can dry seeds in a garage or garden shed that provides the warmth and shelter you require for the task. Make sure to give seeds ample space and time to dry. Spread them out in a thin layer on a surface they will not stick to readily. Stir them regularly to promote uniform drying. Seeds will require anywhere from a few days to up to a few weeks until they are dry enough to store. The larger the seed, the longer it will take. The warmer and dryer the air, which you have some control over, the less time it will take. You may choose to use a food dehydrator, which will work well as long as it does not have a heating element or you have disabled the element.

Seeds can be cleaned after they have dried for a few days, whether they are completely dry or not. The seed chaff is simply easier removed when dry, but the seeds will still require further drying. Here are general ideas and techniques:

▶ **For flowers that produce seed heads:** When the seeds are ripe, the seed head shatters. This is good because it indicates that the seeds are ready, but it is bad because they will shatter whether you have picked them or not, so harvest shattering plants as soon as possible. The seed head will fall apart in your hand when you touch it or attempt to crumble it. You can crumble the plant matter and sift off most seeds using two strainers. The first strainer should allow the seeds and smaller particles to fall through, and the second strainer should allow only the smaller particles through. Zinnias and cosmos are two types of flowers that produce this type of seed head.

▶ **For flowers that have open, rattling pods or seed heads:** Place the pods or seed heads in a large plastic baggie. Seal the baggie, and shake it vigorously until the seeds fall out of the pods. This is another great garden task for the youngest family members. Strain off the debris as mentioned above. Conversely, you can also use the tarp/fan method described in

Chapter 7. Spread the clean seeds onto newsprint or baking sheets to finish drying. Columbine and poppy produce seeds in this manner.

▶ **Tiny seeds:** These dust-like seeds cannot be cleaned with a fan. After putting them through a fine strainer to remove any large pieces of chaff, blow on them very gently while stirring to separate the seeds from the remaining chaff. Be careful to not inhale the particulate matter or get any in your eyes, as it can be very irritating. Campanula and orchid have very fine seeds that must be separated in this manner.

Once they are completely dry, store flower seeds in a cool, dry, dark place like a cold cellar or refrigerator. Some seeds require stratification after harvesting to improve or even allow germination. Daylilies, lilies, and hibiscus, along with many others, are examples of such seeds.

Flowers and Herbs, Alphabetically

Because there are so many flowers in so many families, listing them by family would be a daunting task. And unlike many vegetable and fruit varieties, knowing family characteristics does not generally contribute to knowing what the specific plants in your garden will do. Because most flowers and herbs are self-fertile, self-pollinating, and self-seeding, little care must be taken to produce seed for future generations. You may isolate (generally by bagging or taping in flowers) and hand-pollinate those varieties you wish to preserve pure seed from, but the plants will take care of most of it for you. What follows is a plant-by-plant guide using the common names of the more popular plants used in flower and ornamental gardening.

Ageratum (Ageratum houstonianum)

 This plant is a prolific self-sower, with sand-like seeds in a seed head that is highly prone to shattering. This is one annual that is best placed where you would like it to grow and then left alone to return on its own year after year. The only time you should concern yourself with the seeds are to save and exchange them or to grow more of the flower in other locations. Occasionally, you should also save a batch of seeds to germinate and fill in areas of the ageratum patch that are thinning. Remove seed heads before they are completely dry and place them in a plastic bowl to complete drying and shattering. Sift off the chaff, and store the seeds (which will not require further drying) in a small container like a film canister, with a hole in the top to allow for aeration. This can be kept in the refrigerator or freezer.

Alyssum (Lobularia maritima)

A Brassicaceae family member, alyssum is a cold hardy, early blooming perennial in temperate regions and will self-sow in long growing seasons. It is insect-pollinated, and the fruit is shatter prone. Collect the seeds to dry and store before the fruits break open naturally. They will be easy to open by hand, and the seeds will come out easily by shaking them out. Drying can be done on a paper towel; the seeds will need a cool, dark, dry place to await their planting.

Amaranth (Amaranthus varieties)

This plant is both monoecious and wind pollinated. The separate male and female blooms rely on the wind to fertilize to produce seed. There are hundreds of very tiny seeds contained in the dangling trusses of amaranth. These are clusters similar to grapes. Harvest the trusses when they begin to dry, as the seeds will fall on their own. Set them aside to dry before separating them. Place them in an open container with high sides to keep the wind from blowing them away while they dry. Keep the container in a warm place out of direct sunlight. Once dry, store the seeds in a cool, dark, and dry location.

Astilbe (Astilbe species)

Astilbes are insect-pollinated perennials with pluming feathery flowers. The seedpods are very lightweight and brown when they are ripe for harvesting. To separate out the seeds, rub the seed heads between the palms of your hands over paper. All the pod parts will essentially disintegrate around the seeds, and you may winnow the seeds out. They are ready for immediate storage in a dark, dry, cool place.

Baby's breath (Gypsophila elegans)

This is a common annual used in florist shops across the United States. It is a very delicate plant for a garden and looks lovely in less formal plant arrangements. The white flowers turn brown when they are ready to harvest. Baby's breath is insect-pollinated. The seeds can be found in the center base of the dried flower. Remove them by hand to dry and store. As usual, store them in a cool, dark place until they are to be planted.

Bachelor's button (Centaurea cyanus)

Another cold hardy annual that is cross-pollinated by insects, it can survive mild winters to return a second year, but the gardener should replant this flower's seeds annually. You can harvest seeds when the blooms begin to fade and dry. The seeds are attractive to birds and prone to shattering, so the gardener must get to them early to collect ample seeds. Disassemble the drying flower to reach the seeds at the flower's base. Set them out to dry a few days, and then store them in a cool, dark place.

Basil (Ocimum basilicum)

Basil will cross-pollinate with other varieties. If you are harvesting for seed purity, separate the varieties by at least 150 feet while they are flowering to prevent crossing varieties. These plants grow well in containers, and the containers can be caged or bagged with hand pollination as well. Basil forms seed capsules that contain four seeds each. After the seed capsules dry, harvest, and separate the seeds by hand. Allow them to completely dry, and then locate a cool, dark, dry place to keep them until you are ready to sow them.

Bee balm (Monarda species)

The seeds of the perennial bee balm ripen later in the summer. Seed clusters appear a few weeks after the plant's bloom period is over. Seed heads are ready for harvest when the seeds easily shake from them. Pluck ripe seed heads, and shake them over a plastic bowl to collect them. Leave them in a warm place to complete drying. Drop a packet of desiccant in the bowl, seal it, and store it in the refrigerator until you plant to sow the seeds.

Bellflower *(Campanula species)*

Seedpods of the insect-pollinated bellflower are hidden in the swollen portion of the flower behind its petals. They are prone to shatter and must be harvested prior to being fully dry and ripe. Seed heads can go into a bag to finish ripening and drying before they are dismantled for their seed. Break apart the dry seed heads by hand, and separate out the seeds to store. They should be kept in a cool, dark, dry place until they are to be sown.

Black-Eyed Susan *(Rudbeckia hirta)*

Rudbeckia, the miniature sunflower-like bloom seemingly intended for the smaller garden, is highly attractive to insects, its main pollinator. It has seeds that are ready to harvest when the plant's blooms begin to turn brown and dry. Pluck the seed heads when the petals fall off easily when touched. When they are completely dry, gently crush the heads, and carefully winnow away the chaff, leaving tiny black seeds. The seeds are almost completely dry when the flower is, so there is only a short dry period required before storing them away from light, heat, and humidity.

Borage or starflower (Borago officinalis)

Borage is a plant that is extremely easy to save seed from. When the flowers begin to fade and turn brown, pick the seeds. They easily fall on their own; so get to them before they fall to the ground. Pluck ripe seed heads, and shake them over a plastic bowl to collect them. Leave them in a warm place to complete drying. Drop a packet of desiccant in the bowl, seal it, and store it in the refrigerator until you plant to sow the seeds.

Calendula (Calendula officinalis)

Also called the pot marigold, calendula is very cold hardy. The earlier, double blooming flowers of calendula are often absent of stamen, and therefore sterile, but the second wave of flowers on double bloomers often have stamen with limited fertility. Ensuring adequate insect pollinators (i.e. lots of bees) is the best way to promote ample pollination. Many of the calendula hybrids do not come true from seed, but the standard varieties are easily harvested right before completely maturing on the plant. The seed heads are shatter prone. Pluck them before they open on their own. They will be easy to break open, and the seeds should come out easily when shaken. Dry the seeds a couple days before storing in a cool, dark location.

Canterbury bells (Campanula medium)

There are several variations of Canterbury bells with flowers that differ in shape: bell-shaped, bell-in-bell shaped, and cup-and-saucer shaped. A few varieties are available as annuals, but most are biennial. All have very tiny seeds that are easy to collect by placing dry seed heads into a sandwich-size brown paper bag, allowing them to dry, and then shaking the bag vigorously to separate the seeds from the seed head. Pour out the bag, and separate the seeds away from the debris. Store the dried seed in a cool, dark, and dry location.

Catnip *(Nepeta cataria)*

Catnip is an oft-invasive plant due to its rapid spreading habit. It openly pollinates by insects, and the plentiful seeds spread easily. However, some gardeners choose to cultivate it as it has a wildflower appearance and can be harvested as a drug for pet cats. The catnip's seeds are ready to harvest when the blooms begin to turn brown and dry. Break off the dry seed heads, and gently crush them, carefully winnowing away the chaff. Allow the seeds to dry on a paper towel, and then place them in a cool, dry, dark place to store them until you intend to sow them.

Celosia *(Celosia cristata)*

Celosia plants are monoecious annuals that are wind pollinated, spread easily, and considered weeds in some regions because they end up growing in areas where gardeners do not want them. They are pretty flowers that resemble flames and are edible. Celosia flowers in almost every color possible. They can be harvested when the seed heads are dry, and sifting the seed will separate seed from chaff. Dried seeds can be stored like other seeds, in cool, dark, and dry conditions. Note: Celosia seeds are extremely fine and number approximately 43,000 per ounce. Take care in finding and handling them. Do so in a draft-free place.

China aster (Callistephus chinensis)

If you choose to harvest your own aster seeds, select wilt resistant varieties. The wilt that occurs in aster is seed borne and will pass to successive generations via seed. Aster is an insect-pollinated annual with standard varieties that sometimes cross-pollinate and sometimes self-pollinate. Certain hybrids will not produce reliable seed, which means that the seeds of certain crosses will not grow at all or will have poor germination results. The seeds of these plants are often sterile. The seeds are ripe when the flowers feather like a dandelion.

Capture the entire flower head, and gently crush it to release the seeds. By the time they are ripe and ready for picking, they will only need a couple days of drying. Once dry, store them until you are ready to plant them. Aster is like most plants, and the seeds require dark, dry, cool storage.

Chrysanthemum, or mums (Chrysanthemum)

Mums are grown as annuals, though some gardeners experience success with them as perennials where climates are milder. In Virginia, for example, many mum varieties overwinter for several years and become very large plants. There are many varieties, and they are all cross-pollinated by insects. Harvest seeds from dried seed heads, being careful as they shatter easily. Pluck seed heads that are almost dry, and place them in a brown paper bag to allow them to self-shatter. Shake the bag vigorously to loosen seeds out. You should be able to pour out seeds and flower heads. The seeds will be mostly dried, and will require little additional drying. Store them as with the majority of seeds away from the dangers of humidity, light, and heat.

Clematis (Clematis *species*)

Clematis is a perennial flowering vine that has large, single-blooming flowers. It is insect crossed, but the large, singular, perfect flowers are easy to isolate and pollinate by hand. Clematis seed heads are not prone to shattering, so they may be left on the vine as long as they do not freeze. The seeds must be removed from the seed heads and completely dried instead of being allowed to freeze, as this will destroy the tissue of the seed. Once they are dry, they can be stored in cool or freezing conditions as long as it is dark and dry.

Columbine (Aquilegia *species*)

Lovely columbine is a star-shaped wildflower in parts of Colorado and other subalpine areas. This plant is pollinated by insects, and its petals fall off of their tubular ovaries when the seedpods are nearly matured. The green ovaries resemble five connected bean pods on a stalk. As they ripen and mature, the seedpods begin to brown and the tops open. You can clip them from their stalks at this point, and place them in a paper bag for about a week to finish drying. The seeds fall easily from their pods when is it shaken upside down. There is generally no debris in the tubes, so winnowing will be minimal if needed at all.

Coneflower (Echinacea purpurea)

Coneflowers produce abundant seed from their insect-pollinated flowers, which are attractive to smaller birds. Cut dried seed heads low on their stems. Hang them upside down with a brown sack tied around the stems to dry further. Gently crush the flowers inside the sack, and thresh them. Untie the sack, and pour out the contents to winnow. Seeds will be dry enough to store in a dry, dark, cool location.

Cosmos (Cosmos bipinnatus)

This annual is easily cross-pollinated by insects. Hand pollination and crossing is a favorite pastime of many gardeners, as they are relatively easy to mate and reproduce. In a garden setting, dark flower colors dominate over light ones, and after many successive generations, the light colors will be bred out of the garden. In striped or multicolor varieties, the base color is the dominant color. Bagging is the most successful means of isolation. Harvest the seed heads when they are dry and crush them to remove the seeds. These seeds will be dry enough to store in a dry, dark, cool location.

Coreopsis (Coreopsis varieties)

This is another insect cross-pollinated annual that can be isolated and hand pollinated to preserve pure seed or experiment with hybridization. Numerous colors of coreopsis are available, and the dainty stems and full heads make a beautiful addition to many flower gardens. They are also easily grown in containers in small garden spaces with another plant at their base. Pick almost dry flowers, and remove the petals to isolate the ovary of the plant. Place it in a bag to further dry. When completely dry, pull the ovary apart by hand, and remove the seeds. If they are not quite dry, allow them to dry completely before storing.

Daisy (Asteraceae family)

The many daisies of the Asteraceae family, including English, Gloriosa, Gerbera, and Swan River, are either annual or biennial, and all are insect crossed. All are self-seeding, with some coming true-to-type from seed and others not. It is important to know which of the many varieties you are growing and what specific characteristics it carries. This information is available from the seed grower, or you may have to use an identification key like that from the USDA, available online at **http://plants.usda.gov/**, to find this information. Pick daisy flowers when the petals begin to dry up. Remove and discard the petals, and place the flower heads in a dry paper bag to dry. When they are dry, crush them inside the bag, and shake it vigorously to separate the parts. Pour the bag out, and pick out the seeds from the debris.

Flax (Linum grandiflorum)

Flax is grown both as an ornamental plant and for its fibers and oils. The insect-pollinated flowers give way to a fruit that ripens and dries on the plant before cracking open to self-seed. Harvest the fruits when they are almost completely dried to reveal, and separate the ten seeds in each fruit. Lay the seeds out to dry, and then store them protected from heat, light, and humidity, which will damage the seeds' viability.

Forget-me-not (Myosotis sylvatica)

Forget-me-nots can be grown as an annual or biennial. If it is sown early enough in the spring, the plant will flower the same year, but a late summer planting will produce spring flowers the following year. The forget-me-not is a prolific self-seeding, insect-pollinated plant that returns year after year in most gardens with little effort. To get seeds from forget-me-nots, pluck the flower after it starts to dry. Remove the petals, and discard them. Let the rest of the flower dry. Pull the dry flower apart, and remove the seeds by hand. Further dry the seeds before storing them away from the conditions that are detrimental to most seeds: heat, light, and moisture.

Four-O'clock (Mirabilis family)

Opposite the morning glory, this plant has blooms that open daily in the afternoon. However, it is still insect-pollinated, and individual flowers can be hand-pollinated to produce seed. In temperate climates, it grows as a perennial, but is otherwise an annual. It has tuberous roots that may be dug for overwinter storage in a damp root cellar for replanting in the spring. When crossing four-o'clocks for breeding purposes, it is helpful to note that taller plants are dominant to the dwarf varieties. The fruits of the plant contain one seed each and are attractive to some birds. Pluck the fruit once it is almost dry, and allow it to further dry before opening it to extract the seed. Store the dried seed in a cool, dark location.

Gaillardia (Gaillardia pulchella*)*

The daisy-like flower of the gaillardia ranges from yellow to purple in color. They can be bagged for isolation and hand pollinated, but they will self-seed, so if you grow two varieties in the garden, especially in close proximity, expect them to cross. Similarly to the daisy, pick gaillardia flowers when the petals begin to dry up. Remove and discard the petals, and place the flower heads in a dry paper bag to dry. When they are dry, crush them inside the bag, and shake it vigorously to separate the parts. Pour the bag out, and pick out the seeds from the debris. These separated seeds are ready to store. Choose storage that protects the seeds from light, heat, and humidity for the highest seed viability.

Hollyhock (Alcea rosea*)*

Hollyhock is an annual, perennial, and biennial, depending on the cultivar and region in which it is grown. Annual types must be started early in the long growing season to set seed, and they do not transfer readily, so it is preferred that they are sown where they will grow. Perennial varieties are often grown as biennials, planted from seed, overwintered, and grown a second season for long-grown, mature seeds. All types are insect-pollinated, but the large petals make it possible to hand pollinate and tape the flowers to produce seed selectively. The seeds form in a ring at the flower's base and are compact. The seedpod resembles a membrane-coated miniature lifesaver. The individual seeds are almost black, almost circular, flat discs. When the seedpod is dry on the plant, remove it, and break it open. The seeds will peel out. Separate any seeds that are stuck together by hand, and dry them to store. Hollyhock seeds are not known for long storage life, so plan to use them in next year's garden.

Larkspur (Consolida orientalis)

The annual larkspur was once known as delphinium. Its seeds and saps are poisonous. Regardless, the plant's flowers are beautiful and desirable in the garden. Tall spikes of blue and violet flowers grow above mounds of thin green foliage. Larkspur develops fruits that, once dry, release their seeds from the open end when shaken. Pick seedpods, and shake them over a plastic container. Spread them to dry in a warm location, and then store them safe from warmth, moisture, and damaging light.

Lavender hyssop (Agastache foeniculum)

 Lavender hyssop is a perennial wildflower that grows up to about 3 feet tall with purple spikes of flowers atop a large base of bright green foliage. It has a lovely, minty licorice aroma and is quite attractive in large quantities. Lavender is attractive to insects in any quantity, and that is a good thing because it relies on insects for pollination. The purple flowers fade to brown as they dry. Carefully clip seed heads from their stems to prevent shattering when the stems are nearly dried. When the seed heads are dry, the seeds will fall easily from the heads. Gentle threshing is appropriate. The seeds should be ready for storage in a cool, dark place as they are extracted.

Lilacs (Syringa vulgaris)

These gorgeous, showy, flowering bushes with compact bunches of small blossoms emit one of the most beloved and familiar fragrances in the world and are as attractive to their insect pollinators as they are to humans. Flowering among the various species of lilac occurs between mid-spring and early summer. The fruit is presented as a dry, brown capsule, which splits in half at maturity and releases two winged seeds, similar to those of maple trees. The seeds can be collected after release and are ready for immediate storage in a dark, dry, cool location.

Lobelia (Lobelia erinus)

Lobelia is a border plant, a low-laying insect-pollinated ground cover that is also used in containers, trailing over the sides. Generally, it is a blue flower, but white lobelia is also common. The capsulated seeds are mist fine, and harvesting is best done by putting the dry capsules in a plastic bag, cracking them, and shaking them vigorously. Do not store the seeds in the plastic bag as condensation may build up and cause the seeds to rot before you can plant them.

Lupine (Lupinus perennis)

Lupines range in variety from small annual wildflowers up to hardy perennial shrubs that grow up to 10 feet tall. They have soft green foliage and insect-pollinated flower spikes that come in various blue and purple shades. Ripened seedpods of the lupine begin to yellow, and the seeds rattle loosely inside when they are ready to pick. Dry, and gently thresh the seeds. They are ready for immediate storage, which must be in a cool to cold, dark, dry location.

Mallow, Rose **(Lavatera trimestris)**

 Rose mallow is a close relative to the hollyhock and bears resemblance to it as well. It is insect-pollinated, like most garden flower varieties. Mallow also produces its seed in a pod, but unlike hollyhock, there is only one seed per seedpod. The seedpods are ready to harvest from when they are nearly completely dried on the stem. Remove the pod, and open it by hand to extract the seed. Allow the seeds to dry further, and then store them until time to germinate. Storage should be like most other seeds — dark, cool, and dry.

Marigold **(Tagetes patula** *and* **tenuifolia)**

Follow the same recommendations for marigold as you would for the coneflower, except you may need smaller sacks because the flower heads are somewhat smaller with more delicate stems. Cut dried seed heads low on their stems. Hang them upside down with a brown sack tied around the stems to dry further. Gently crush the flowers inside the sack, and thresh them. Untie the sack, and pour out the contents to winnow. Marigolds produce abundant seed as well. Store these in paper envelopes in a dark, dry, cool location.

Morning glory **(Ipomoea purpurea)**

Morning glory is a prolific vining plant with blue flowers that open in the early morning and close by the afternoon. The flowers have five connected petals in a disc shape. Insect-pollinated, morning glory flowers may require help to successfully pollinate as they are not open all day and for days on end like many other flowers. The globe-shaped fruit of the morning glory usually contains about six developed seeds. Open the seedpods to dry these seeds before storing in a cool, dark, dry location. Note: The seeds that result from the vining plant require scarification to germinate through their hard shells.

Nasturtium (Trapaeolum majus)

Long used as a breeding plant to obtain different colors and characteristics, countless cultivars of nasturtium are available. The plant has disc-shaped green leaves and usually orange, red, or yellow flowers that strongly resemble those of the hibiscus, but smaller. Nasturtium has a low-growing, vining tendency. It does not get very tall, but provides excellent ground cover. The entire plant is edible. Each fruit the plant produces contains three seeds, and it is easiest to harvest these seeds by extracting them by hand. The seeds are best dried before storage, and like most other seeds, should be stored in a cool, dark, and dry place.

Painted tongue (Salpiglossis sinuata)

Painted tongue is often referred to as trumpet flower, as the petals flare like the end of a trumpet. The flowers bloom above a long, thin stalk, with long, thin, green flowers. The plants usually sprout up to a couple feet tall — rarely more — with variegated (striped) blooms in many color combinations. Painted tongue is open pollinated by insects, and so care should be taken to avoid crossing if you are looking for specific colors to remain in your garden. Otherwise, allow them to pollinate freely. As the blooms fade, a seedpod forms. Once the seedpod browns, cut it off. Allow it to completely dry before cracking it open to remove the hundreds of sandy seeds. They will not require drying if stored in a container with a silica gel that will draw out any remaining moisture. Like most seeds, storage should be cool, dry, and dark.

Pansy (Viola species)

The pansy is another species that may be grown as an annual, perennial, or biennial. Various cultivars are early blooming, some survive warmer summers, and others are frost, and even snow, resistant. Pansy is cross-pollinated, but it can self-pollinate as well. Pansies grow fruit seed capsules that should be handpicked and set aside in a small cardboard box. As the fruits dry, they eject their own seed. This usually occurs on the plant, so if you carefully examine the soil, you should see the tiny seeds resting on the surface of the soil. Collect as many as possible to dry and store in a dry, dark, cool place.

Petunia (Petunia species)

Petunia is an annual that is insect-pollinated and highly desired by breeders who have successfully bred flowers that bloom more abundantly than the traditional cultivars. Petunia commonly self-seeds (at least the non-sterile hybrids do). The later blooming flowers set better seed in most cases. The fruits are handpicked and opened dry to remove the few hundred tiny seeds inside. Crushing one seed will determine how dry it is. If it is still soft, supple, and crushes easily, it is not completely dry. Once the seed you test is dry, store the rest of the seeds in a location free from humidity and heat.

Phlox (**Phlox drummondii**)

Phlox is a low-lying, soft, and airy ground covering that spreads well. It has clusters of tiny flowers that comprise the range of red, blue, lavender, and white colors. Most phlox self-pollinates. The tiny flowers are generally not attractive to bees or other insects. Each mature phlox fruit produces three seeds. Remove the almost-dry fruit from the plant, and crush it gently to remove the seeds. Dry them before storing in a cool, dark, dry place.

Poppy (**Papaver somniferum**)

This plant is the annual, insect-pollinated variety of the plant popularized in *The Wizard of Oz* by Frank L. Baum. It is also a controversial plant, as its sap is harvested for use in opiate drugs. Poppy seeds are also edible, commonly used to bake with. Pick poppy flowers when the petals begin to dry up. Remove and discard the petals, and place the flower heads in a dry paper bag to dry. When they are dry, crush them inside the bag, and shake it vigorously to separate the parts. Pour the bag out, and pick out the small black seeds from the debris. Store these seeds in containers in a location that is low in humidity and cool.

Primrose (**Primula** *species*)

Primrose is an elegant, simple flower, which usually has a corolla of five heart-shaped petals in white, yellow, purple, or red. The flowers are beautiful, edible, and are used in teas. Its seed is extremely fine. The capsules containing the seeds are closed until they are ready for harvesting. Examining the capsules daily will reveal ones that are beginning to open and ready to harvest. As the seeds are extremely fine, they require little time to dry thoroughly and are ready to store soon after harvesting.

Sage, culinary varieties (Salvia officinalis)

Sage is a fragrant herb that has long, thin, silvery green leaves and presents blue or purple flowers. The leaves are very commonly used as herbs, but the flowers also are edible. Sage, like other members of the Salvia family, is insect-pollinated. When the seed heads of sage are completely brown and dry, gently crush them, and carefully winnow off the chaff, leaving the seeds to be dried and stored in a cool, dark, arid location.

Snapdragon (Antirrhinum majus)

Snapdragon is another perennial that is often grown as an annual, as it is not cold hardy. It can be propagated from cuttings dipped in rooting hormones and placed in the soil. Generally, snapdragon self-pollinates, so crossing would take a deliberate effort, which has been made by many breeders with a variety of hybridizations resulting. You can harvest the individual fruits from the stalks as they ripen. The seeds are exceptionally tiny, and each of the ripened fruits contains many seeds. It will take some effort to separate out the seeds from the rest of the flower. Using a tool like a tiny flathead screwdriver or a metal spatula may help the dividing process. Dry the seeds completely, then store them in a cool, dry location until you are ready to plant them.

Sunflowers (Helianthus annuus *and* cucumerifolius)

Sunflowers are out breeding and will cross-pollinate. They must be isolated by ½ mile from other varieties to ensure pure seed. Plant several of each variety to promote good genetic variation. Before you harvest the plant's head, it must be dry and browning, and the petals must be able to drop with a touch. Birds enjoy sunflower seeds as much as humans, if not more. You can cut the blooms off and hang them by their stems, which should be protected by paper grocery sacks, to dry out before shelling the seeds by hand. Dry the seeds on a sheet of newsprint or a length of thin fabric out of direct sunlight. Keep dried seeds you intend for planting in a low-moisture, cool location.

Sweet pea (Lathyrus odoratus)

The sweet pea plant is a self-pollinating annual climbing vine. It is a recommended plant for the beginning breeder because it is easily taped and crossed in the same manner a cucurbit would be. Male anthers are pollen-ripe before the female stigmas are receptive, but the time between these points are negligible. You can apply the pollen as soon as it is ready, and as soon as the stigma is receptive, it will fertilize. Make sure to reseal the fertilized flowers and mark them with tape or pipe cleaners around the stem to harvest for seed later. After the pea pods ripen and begin to dry on the vine, pluck them to completely dry before you split them open and remove the seeds. The seeds will likely need further drying before storing, as they are relatively large and do not dry as quickly as smaller seeds often do. They should be completely dry and placed in an airtight container with a moisture absorber, like silica gel, to preserve them best. The container should be stored in a cool, dark location, like a refrigerator vegetable drawer.

Tobacco or Nicotiana **(Nicotiana alata)**

This is a long-blooming perennial in temperate regions that is often grown as an annual. Nicotiana is a pretty, smaller garden plant that is also a crop. It sows itself by shattering its numerous seeds. The seeds are about as small as salt or sugar granules. Crush the seedpod that forms at the base of the bloom gently to reveal the hundreds of tiny seeds inside. Tobacco seeds dry quickly once they are removed from the pods, so plan to store them soon after harvesting in a cool, dark, dry location.

Verbena **(Verbena species)**

Verbena is an all-season perennial bloomer with dense heads of tiny, five-petal flowers appearing in shades of blues and lavenders, and sometimes whites and pinks. The plant has a bushing tendency and can be as short as 6 inches or tall as 3 feet, with 1- to 3-inch flowers. Verbena is insect-pollinated. Each fruit is composed of a cluster of "nutlets" that each contain a single seed, and these nutlets are harvested when almost completely dry. The nutlets are opened by hand to extract the seed. Like most seeds, the seeds of the verbena must be dried thoroughly before storing in cool, dark conditions, free of excess humidity, until they are ready to plant.

Zinnia (Zinnia elegans)

Annual zinnias cross-pollinate by insects. Gardeners should only grow one variety at a time to save pure seed or should isolate varieties by ¼ mile. Dry, brown flowers indicate the seeds are ready to harvest. The seeds are contained in the very center and are somewhat tenacious to remove. Crush the flowers to remove the seeds.

Self-Sowing Annual Quick Reference

Like perennials, self-sowing annuals come back every year. But they come back with different variations and crosses and from seeds instead of established roots. They are significantly less predictable than perennials are. The seed dispersal, or spread, of an annual that self-seeds can be wide and uneven. Some patches can be thick; others thin, and sometimes they do not come back at all when you would want them to.

So why choose annuals with all the unpredictability they present?

▶ They are a cost-effective alternative to buying expensive seed or plants.

▶ They fill in the gaps between the plants you planted on purpose and make your garden look lush.

▶ If you do not like them, you can pull them up any time and not feel too guilty.

▶ If you do not like them where they are, you may be able to move them.

▶ They do all the work — collecting, drying, storing, stratifying, sowing, and transplanting — for you.

Self-sowing annuals

- Alyssum
- Amaranth
- Annual clary sage
- Bells of Ireland
- Blue woodruff
- Bupleurum
- Calendula
- California poppy
- Cerinthe
- Chinese forget-me-not
- Cleome
- Coreopsis tinctoria
- Cornflower
- Cosmidium
- Cosmos
- Feverfew
- Flowering tobacco
- Four-o'clock
- Lavatera
- Malva 'zebrina'
- Morning glory
- Night-scented stock
- Oenothera 'Sunset Boulevard'
- Pincushion flower
- Poppy
- Rudbeckia
- Snapdragon
- Sweet pea
- Verbena bonariensis
- Viola

CHAPTER 11:
Getting Things Started

Every plant has its beginning. From seed to seed, you will need to take many steps to get the seeds you have chosen for your garden to grow, blossom, and produce seeds for years to come. You can collect seed from the plants you already have in the ground or those you buy or start from seed yourself. Once you have the seeds you want to grow in hand, you will need a variety of techniques to help them produce the dried pods, plumes, and heads of seeds that will produce the next year's garden. This chapter explores the various methods for getting your seeds off to the right start, beginning with preparing the seed to go into the soil. Then you will learn how to protect them at their early, vulnerable stages and how to move them to where they will finish out their lives and deliver your seed harvest to you.

Seed Scarification

Scarification is altering the seed coat to allow air and water into the seed, which initiates germination. Many perennials and woody plant seeds cannot absorb water through their seed coats. Others have seed coats that do not allow oxygen and other gases to pass through, and the seed produces these gases as it metabolizes its energy stores and required to germinate. Though some seed coats eventually decompose enough to germinate on their own, scarification can speed germination, putting the plant on the gardener's timeline.

There are several methods of scarification: mechanical filing, abrasion with sandpaper, boiling the seed in water, or chemical degradation with a concentrated sulfuric acid compound, which is generally done by commercial growers on a large scale and not usually required by the home gardener. Scarification should be conducted carefully to avoid damaging the internal tissues of a seed. Each type of seed will have suggested best methods for their individual scarification, and you should always check with the producers or growers to determine which to use. What follows is a brief description of the two scarification methods home gardeners generally use.

▶ **Mechanical scarification:** Using your knowledge of the anatomy of seeds from Chapter 4, select a place on the seed away from the embryo and cut, file, or sand through the seed coat until you begin to see cotyledons. In this way, you are exposing enough of the seed so that it may begin the process of germination.

▶ **Water scarification:** In order to scarify with water, you will want to put the seeds in a container that will not melt, as you will be pouring boiling water over the seeds. The water expands and opens the tiny, otherwise impermeable pores that exist in the seed coat. The process generally requires you leave the seed in the hot water, which will cool over time. As the pores open, the water will seep into the seed and cause the tissue inside to expand within the softened seed coat, creating tiny tears in it that will allow the germination process to continue.

Seed Stratification

The seeds that you extract from the fruit of temperate zone fruit trees, as well as many flowers, need to pass through a period of colder temperatures. During this cold period, the seeds complete critical stages of growth needed to germinate. When seeds are planted in the fall and grow outdoors, they are naturally subjected to the cold temperatures that occur during the winter months before they germinate. If you plan to bypass the fall planting and plant inside in the early spring or outside after frost (or even after storing them for a couple years), you will need to artificially reproduce the cold conditions for the seeds. The process for creating these cold conditions is called **stratification.**

Essentially, you will be fooling your seeds into thinking that it is time for them to germinate but without having to go through the usual lengthy procedure that would have to take place in nature. To do this:

▶ Soak the seeds in lukewarm water for 12 hours, and then plant each seed in small watertight containers of damp potting soil.

▶ The containers should have lids so that they can be closed. Place the containers in the refrigerator where the temperature should be not cold enough to freeze, but not exceeding 50 degrees.

▶ Depending on where you live and the date of the last expected frost of the year, plan on leaving your containers of seeds in the fridge for approximately three to four months before the intended date of transplanting.

▶ During that time, make sure that the containers are not too cold (as in freezing) and that each seed has begun to take root. You should be able to see the roots starting to press up against the sides of the containers if you look closely.

▶ Make sure that the soil in each container is kept consistently moist, but not too wet.

Starting Outdoors

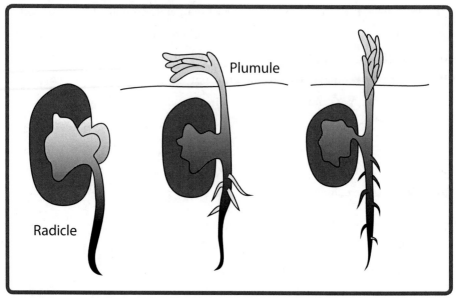

Germination of a seed

Depending on the part of the country in which you live, you can set up a seed nursery, either indoors or out. The tropical climate in the southernmost parts of the United States makes it possible to take your seeds from the germination stage to mature plants while being kept entirely outside during that time period. Those in northern climates must start seeds indoors, waiting for frost dangers to pass before making the transplanting transition to the outdoors. Even if you live in the more tropical zones and are able to start your seeds outdoors, bear in mind that some sort of protection from the elements will still be necessary during the crucial germination phase and while the plants are still tender. Germination occurs when the outer covering of the seed cracks open so the embryonic plant that is within the seed can send the root of the plant deeper into the soil. This is also when the upper part of the plant breaks the surface of the soil. Due to the fragility of the new seedlings, it is important that they are not drowned and crushed by a sudden downpour, or burned by a too hot sun.

The United States Department of Agriculture has divided the United States into 11 different climate zones. Using average low winter temperatures as a guide, each zone is 10 degrees Fahrenheit colder or warmer than the one next to it. Each gardening zone of the country has its own criteria for when to plant. While it is possible to deviate from these rules, remember that these guidelines are there to help you to avoid losing any plants due to exposure to temperatures that are too cold or the lingering possibility of frost, especially in the northern regions. Following these zone paradigms will help ensure that all your plants have every chance to grow and develop to the best of their ability.

TABLE 11: CHART OF GARDENING ZONES FOR NORTH AMERICA

Zone	Fahrenheit	Celsius	Example Cities
1	Below -50	Below -45.6	Fairbanks, AK; Resolute, Northwest Territories (CAN)
2a	-50 to -45	-42.8 to -45.5	Prudhoe Bay, AK; Flin Flon, Manitoba (CAN)
2b	-45 to -40	-40.0 to -42.7	Unalakleet, AK; Pinecreek, MN
3a	-40 to -35	-37.3 to -39.9	International Falls, MN; St. Michael, AK
3b	-35 to -30	-34.5 to -37.2	Tomahawk, WI; Sidney, MT
4a	-30 to -25	-31.7 to -34.4	Minneapolis/St.Paul, MN; Lewistown, MT
4b	-25 to -20	-28.9 to -31.6	Northwood, IA; Nebraska
5a	-20 to -15	-26.2 to -28.8	Des Moines, IA; Illinois
5b	-15 to -10	-23.4 to -26.1	Columbia, MO; Mansfield, PA
6a	-10 to -5	-20.6 to -23.3	St. Louis, MO; Lebanon, PA
6b	-5 to 0	-17.8 to -20.5	McMinnville, TN; Branson, MO
7a	0 to 5	-15.0 to -17.7	Oklahoma City, OK; South Boston, VA
7b	5 to 10	-12.3 to -14.9	Little Rock, AR; Griffin, GA
8a	10 to 15	-9.5 to -12.2	Tifton, GA; Dallas, TX

8b	15 to 20	-6.7 to -9.4	Austin, TX; Gainesville, FL
9a	20 to 25	-3.9 to -6.6	Houston, TX; St. Augustine, FL
9b	25 to 30	-1.2 to -3.8	Brownsville, TX; Fort Pierce, FL
10a	30 to 35	1.6 to -1.1	Naples, FL; Victorville, CA
10b	35 to 40	4.4 to 1.7	Miami, FL; Coral Gables, FL
11	above 40	above 4.5	Honolulu, HI; Mazatlan, Mexico

While it is definitely an advantage to be able to start your seeds outdoors and to not have to sacrifice space inside, each situation has its own pros and cons. Practically every type of seed will benefit from a close watch at this stage no matter if they are started indoors or out. Plants that are started outdoors must be carefully attended to and checked periodically for any signs of distress. Temperature fluctuations can be deadly, and an unexpected thunderstorm or freeze can wreak havoc on young plants. Because they are outside, they are more susceptible to disease, insect invasion, and nightly critter raids. In order to protect your precious flats and containers against the unpredictable rigors of the outdoors, you must have a place to keep them that will offer shelter and protection.

Getting the Inside Edge

It would be wonderful to have ample space in a perfectly climate controlled environment to successfully produce a crop of perfect seeds that would become perfect plants. If you are lucky to have a sun porch, which is a room off the main part of the house that is enclosed by glass, or any room that is well lit by large windows and doors, you have the means to set up a temporary indoor greenhouse. However, unless you have a specific area of your house or garage that can be dedicated to your efforts, the reality is that for the time it takes, you will have to sacrifice a certain amount of precious indoor space.

Placing flats and containers on windowsills has always been the method of starting seeds and plants. For those with young children, pets, or even clumsy spouses or roommates, this situation could present problems like accidental spills. One misplaced elbow or bump of a tail and your seeds and their containers and soil will become nothing more than a mess of organic matter to throw on the compost heap. There is no way to locate and separate out tiny seeds that get knocked over and mixed up with others.

There is a more suitable (and safer) way to start plants indoors, if you have the room. Small tables, or even makeshift tables composed of pieces of plywood stretched across two sawhorses, can be placed in front of those windowsills to provide a better way to get the same light with more space. This also gives you a slightly more secure location, eliminating some of the concern about the animals or kids knocking over the various containers. As long as you keep in mind that it is only a temporary and seasonal thing, it should not put too much of a crimp in the household routine.

Seeing Things in the Right Light

While some seeds demand bright light for germination, others do better if they are covered or kept in the dark until they have popped through the surface of the soil. Most vegetable seeds have been shown to perform just as well either way, but some flower seeds need darkness to germinate. If you are germinating several varieties of seeds in one place at the same time, you can use sheets of newspaper to cover the flats of seeds that need darkness during the daylight hours, or for the hours that you are administering artificial light. This allows all the flats to reach the transplanting stage and be ready to go outdoors at approximately the same time.

In the same respect, because they are living, breathing organisms, plants need their rest. Because photosynthesis only occurs during daylight hours, a plant's metabolic systems slow down during the hours of darkness. However, when it is dark, plants are still growing, and the leaves are producing carbohydrates, which are the main ingredient in the growth process. Ideally, for most plants requiring light for germination, aim to expose the flats to approximately 16 hours of light, natural or otherwise, during a 24-hour period. If you are starting out in early spring, the shorter daylight hours and the implications from this guideline necessitate providing as much natural daylight as is possible and even possibly supplementing with a few hours of fluorescent light, if you have the equipment to do so.

The following seeds germinate better in darkness:

▶ Centuria	▶ Pansy	▶ Portulaca
▶ Larkspur	▶ Phlox	▶ Verbena

These seeds can germinate in either lightness or darkness:

▶ Alyssum	▶ Cosmos	▶ Pepper
▶ Aster	▶ Cucumber	▶ Squash
▶ Balsam	▶ Dahlia	▶ Tomato
▶ Broccoli	▶ Dianthus	▶ Vinca
▶ Cabbage	▶ Eggplant	▶ Watermelon
▶ Cauliflower	▶ Marigold	▶ Zinnia
▶ Celosia	▶ Muskmelon	

Until the seeds have broken the surface of the soil mix, the soil should be misted at least once every day with distilled water until it feels moist to the touch. Once the seeds have sprouted and have begun to grow, they should be slowly and gently watered each day. Be careful not to overwater, as this is an easy mistake to make and one of the quickest ways to potentially cause the germinating seeds to grow moldy or rot before they have a chance to push through the soil.

Other Indoor Alternatives

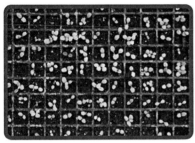

Tray of seedlings

If space limitations or the habits of your family and pets do not allow you to put your flats and containers in front of the windows, there are countless alternatives. Any place that will accommodate as many tables or sawhorses as it takes to hold the containers will suffice. As long as you have a way to hang a fluorescent light or two over those same tables in the basement or any other out of the way spot, you can make room for your trays of newly planted seeds that will hopefully germinate into healthy **seedlings**, which is the term for the first young plants that sprout. Some clever gardeners have been known to clear off shelves in the pantry for their flats of sprouting seeds or to keep them in the bathtub of a rarely used guest bathroom. Gardeners know only too well that necessity is the mother of invention.

Scientifically speaking, the term "room temperature" refers to a range of temperatures from 68 to 77 degrees Fahrenheit, as determined by the United States Metric Association. The majority of American homes in the winter and cooler months fall in the lower half of this range. These temperatures are warm enough for most seeds to germinate and mature far enough to be transplanted. Seeds generally prefer warm conditions to germinate, so if you are planning to start seeds indoors, the warmer the temperature, the better (74 to 77 degrees). If you keep a very cool home, the germination process can be helped along considerably if the soil temperature of your flats is artificially raised to be higher than the temperature in which you yourself feel comfortable. If possible, keep a space heater close by the flats and containers to bring the air temperature up because this will shorten the length of time it takes for the seeds to sprout. It is important to remember to provide the proper amount of light, consistent temperatures, good ventilation, and adequate moisture (particularly if using artificial heating processes), which will give your seeds the conditions they need to germinate and flourish.

Once they have sprouted and the dangers you are avoiding by growing them indoors (freezing, harsh weather, or predators) have passed, your plants are going to be ready to transplant outdoors. The next chapter covers that process in depth, but generally, you will be ready to do so within two to three weeks.

Part of the appeal of gardening is that it is such a basic, primal activity. You do not really need a lot of fancy equipment to garden. Some of the most elementary items used in gardening have been around a long time, and they serve their purpose just fine. In that regard, greenhouses, cold frames, and garden cloches are all simplistic, yet highly effective, tools for the gardener who needs to offer some extra protection to his or her plants at any specific time.

Gardeners in the northern zones (from zones 5 to 1) will find more use for cold frames and cloches than those that garden in the zones 6 to 11. This is not to say that southern gardeners cannot enjoy the benefits of using them, but it is more likely that a gardener in Iowa would need a cold frame more than someone in Florida. A greenhouse, on the other hand, is an item that any serious gardener in any zone would love to have.

If you ask a serious gardener what is at the top of his or her gardening wish list, the most likely answer you will get is some sort of a greenhouse. Whether you have an enormous garden or just a small collection of containers on a patio, as a gardener, you might still dream of being able to walk up and down and putter among those tables of every type of plant imaginable. A greenhouse gives the gardener ultimate control over the plants that he or she can grow. The climate in a greenhouse can be artificially controlled to bring the temperature up to the tropical conditions necessary for year-round orchid cultivation, or it can be brought down to the cool temperatures that are desired for seed germination and seedling maintenance. In many instances, the only way some gardeners can enjoy their hobby is within the confines of a greenhouse. This is especially true for those who do not have access to any other environment or those who prefer to garden indoors.

Greenhouses can be as small as a 3-foot by 3-foot plastic terrarium, able to hold just a few specimens, or they can be full size glass structures, tall enough and with enough room within to support trees and shrubs. There is a wide diversity among the available types of greenhouses. Regardless the size, greenhouses are a suitable alternative to starting your seeds outdoors. In addition to simulating the appropriate climate for germination, you can lengthen the growing season and get a head start by starting seedlings inside a greenhouse well before they would be able to be started outdoors. This is exceptionally useful in regions with short growing seasons and can even increase the variety of plants a gardener can grow. Say, for example, a plant takes 28 warm-weather weeks to produce a fruit, but you only get 24 warm weather weeks in your region. Starting in a greenhouse and transplanting in about the fifth week will give you the right conditions to get fruit from the plant that would otherwise give you none.

Places, Please

Preparing for Transplanting Outdoors

After your seedlings' roots have taken hold and the plants themselves have developed a mature set of leaves, they are ready to be transplanted. Usually, the first two leaves a seedling produces are its false leaves. They are actually the cotyledons that formed inside the seed and matured during germination. They will shrivel and die after the first real, or true, leaves form. The false leaves will likely not even resemble the shape of the plants real leaves. Once the real leaves develop and strengthen, the plant is ready to be moved to transplant (again, if the weather is cooperating). This can take anywhere from two weeks to a month.

In many cases, you will be transplanting the new seedlings into slightly larger containers and flats before they make the eventual journey to their new home outdoors. If you are moving the new plants into a larger flat, it is a good idea to give them some additional support by using plant bands. You can construct plant bands out of old newspaper. The following instructions will help you band your plants properly without damaging them.

Making a plant band

You will need newspaper, tape, and a small jar.

1. Lay the jar on its side.

2. Loosely wrap the newsprint around the sides and bottom of the jar, taping the sides and bottom to secure them. Leave the top open.

3. Slide the newsprint off the jar. This is a plant band.

4. Position your plant bands inside the flats you will use for the next stage of transplanting. The flat is the shallow, rectangular, plastic tray that holds starter pots or plant bands. It usually has a lot of drainage.

5. Push the plant bands down side-by-side in your prepared flats, and then fill them with potting mix. Put the new plants in the potting mix to help to keep the seedlings' roots separated, and provide the recommended nourishment to each one.

6. After you have filled each band with an individual plant, cover the remainder of the area with more potting medium, and tamp it down around each plant. These little newsprint pots will decay as time goes by.

7. When you get ready to move the plant to either the outdoors or another container, you can peel away and discard whatever is left of these at the time of planting.

When you are ready to move your plants into their plant bands within the new flats or containers, very carefully use a small tool that will get the new plant out without disturbing or damaging the one next to it. Most of the gardening tools that you are familiar with, such as hand-held trowels and weeders, are too large and cumbersome to accomplish this safely. Anything that is long and narrow enough to get underneath and lift each seedling out without pulling up too much of accompanying dirt will work just fine. One useful tool is a small, cake-icing spatula, available in most kitchen stores and hobby supply stores, or even an old butter knife you can get for pennies at a thrift store. You want to bring up as much of the new root system as possible with the least amount of damage.

Carefully plant each individual seedling before removing another, as it is not good for the fragile new roots to be exposed to the air for too long. Be careful how you handle them; take care not to touch the stems any more than necessary, and, if possible, try to support the root system in the palm of your hand while you work.

Hardening Off

Once your plants have matured enough and have reached the stage where they are finally ready to be transplanted outdoors, they will need to be hardened off so that the shock of being in the outdoor environment and the unpredictable elements will not adversely affect them. **Hardening off** is moving your immature plants outdoors for a certain length of time each day, gradually increasing their exposure to the harsher outdoor conditions. They gradually will become sturdy enough to be planted outdoors without being distressed because the stems and leaves of the seedlings literally will become harder and thicker, and this will make them less susceptible to damage when moved outdoors. When the outside temperatures in your area are consistently above 50 degrees in the daytime hours, you can begin the hardening off process.

Start at least a week before you plan on transplanting. During the week before you start the hardening off process, decrease the amount of water and fertilizer that your plants have been getting, and if possible, move them to a location that is slightly cooler than where they have been. After a week, you can then move them outside. Every day, move them to a protected spot that preferably has indirect light and not too much wind. If you have a cold frame, this is the perfect time to use it. *See Chapter 6 for more information about cold frames.*

Hardening off process

About a week before transplanting:

▶ Start decreasing water and fertilizer. Water only every two days or so.

▶ While they are still in their containers outdoors, water sparingly and fertilize once.

▶ Keep increasing the time the plants are outdoors until finally you are only bringing them in a night. If you notice signs of stress, like wilting, make sure to bring them inside. The idea is to expose them as long as possible to reduce the stress they will experience when they are finally put outside altogether.

▶ After a week of temperatures that are consistently above freezing at night, you can leave them outdoors all day and overnight.

▶ Once they have been outdoors for three days and nights in a row, you can finally transplant them into the ground.

While they are in the cold frame or other protected area, make sure that the soil in their pots is kept moist, but do not overwater. Hardening off should take about a week, and after this phase in their young lives is complete, your plants are ready to take the big step into their new homes in your garden.

Transplanting

After your plants have been hardened off for a week or so, it is time to move them to their final destination in the garden. That may mean planting them directly into the ground or into a container of some sort. No matter where they end up, it is wise to make sure that conditions are favorable before taking them out of their plant-band containers and putting them anywhere outside. By now, the plants have been exposed to the weather enough to be able to withstand the prevailing natural state. However, because they are still vulnerable during the transplantation stage, do not put them in the ground if it is too hot, or if the sun is beating down on them.

If there is a lot of sunshine on the day that you intend to transplant, plant during the early morning hours, or in the evening instead, when it is cooler. Plant each plant individually, and water gently as you go. As when you were taking the tiny seedlings out of the soil for their original transplanting, be extra careful with the roots, as any harm to them at this crucial stage of their lives could cause permanent damage.

Always be aware of the last frost dates in your area, and be prepared to take measures to protect your new plants if needed. Nothing is more disappointing to a gardener than losing a crop of newly planted seedlings after months of babying them along, especially if they have been grown from seed. Take action against weather by placing protection over your plants. You can use any number of everyday objects; anything that will fit over the plants without suffocating them (jars or bowls) will work well. If you have any of those beautiful glass garden cloches, discussed in Chapter 6, now is the time to use them.

Once they are transplanted, keep careful watch over the seedlings for any signs of distress, such as wilting or yellowing of stems or leaves. This is often referred to as shock. Just as if you went from a comfortable house directly into a hot tub for a few hours and then while wet, back in to the air conditioning, a plant experiences a great deal of change when it is transplanted from one climate to another. While it is natural and expected that a certain amount of drooping will occur over the next few days, make sure your plants' transitions are as easy for them as possible, keeping them shaded if they wilt heavily. Remember not to overwater. It is tempting and you might feel the urge to water them beyond what is necessary, but curb that impulse. The idea is to keep them moist, not wet; cool, not cold or hot; undisturbed; and protected.

Transplanting New Fruit Trees

When it comes time to plant the sprouted seeds, you can either take them directly outdoors if the danger of frost is past, or — if the weather is not cooperating — move the seedlings into temporary housing until it warms up outside. You can use some waxed cardboard beverage containers, such as milk or juice cartons, and cut them down to form little square pots in which to plant your little fruit tree seedlings. This method is beneficial because when it comes time to transplant your seedlings, all you need to do is to slice down each corner of the container, pull it open from each side, and then set it into the hole you have dug for each seed. Once the containers are planted, the natural action of the elements upon the organic material of the containers will cause them to deteriorate in time without any undue stress on the roots of the fledging fruit tree.

In order to give your new trees the best possible opportunity to grow and bear luscious fruit, make sure that the new seedlings are planted in soil that is well drained and maintains a constant neutral pH level.

To transplant your fruit tree outdoors:

▸ Put each tree into a hole that is approximately 6 inches deep, and make sure that the soil in the hole is loose and crumbly.

▸ Make a mound of dirt inside the hole so that the developing roots will have support.

▸ Add a cupful of compost down into the hole, and water the compost until it is uniformly wet.

▸ Place the new seedling into the hole, and then fill up the hole with dirt so that the new tree is actually sitting slightly above the level of the ground.

▸ Mulch around the bottom of the trees with a compost of dead leaves and straw, as this will serve to fertilize them as well as to help keep weed growth down to a minimum.

▸ Once the new seedlings have reached a height of more than 2 feet, you might want to stake them so that they grow straight and vertical. When doing this, take care to avoid using anything that might possibly cut into the tender new bark of the young tree. Using ties of soft cloth or pantyhose to tether the saplings to their stakes should do the trick nicely. Be careful not to tie them up too tightly, as the trunk will need room to expand as it grows.

Do not mulch all the way up to the trunk of the tree, as cutting off the air supply to the trunk could cause the bark to rot if it gets too wet. Leave a few inches between the mulch and the tree to ensure that the trunk dries out properly between watering. Peach, nectarine, and apricot trees can get to be as high as 20 feet tall. While the trees are maturing, only prune them if necessary, as pruning will inhibit the amount of fruit that they produce. Check your new trees regularly for signs of insect infestation or evidence that deer or other critters are gnawing through the bark. If you find that this is happening, you can create a barrier by wrapping a sleeve of chicken wire or metal screening — both of these materials can be purchased at any garden or hardware store — around the bottom of the trunk of the tree, up to the height on the trunk where you can tell the damage begins. This will prevent whatever animal is causing the damage from being able to get access to the tasty bark.

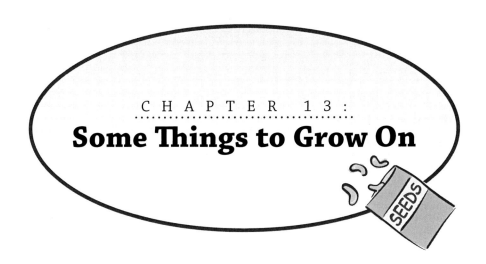

C H A P T E R 1 3 :
Some Things to Grow On

Soil Basics 101

It might seem like a no-brainer, but one of the most important elements in growing healthy plants and their future healthy seeds is a good soil mixture. It is essential that you understand this process while planning where and how you intend to plant your garden. It is interesting to note that in getting seeds started, very little is needed in the way of actual soil quality. As long as the plants are receiving the proper air, water, and light requirements, they should germinate, sprout, and flourish. You will not need to supplement the soil in any way until the seedlings have sprouted, begun to grow, and require more in the way of nutrition. One of the earliest lessons a gardener should learn is how to leave well enough alone. Too often gardeners become so preoccupied with worrying about the well-being of their plants that they tend to overwater and add too much fertilizer when most plants are perfectly happy with the minimum requirements.

Try not to get caught up in the trap of loving your plants to death. Too much of anything is not a good thing. As long as the plants have sufficient water, light, and are in a decent growing medium, they will be fine.

A good way to make a homemade soil medium is to mix together three parts commercial topsoil and one part each of peat moss and cow manure. Peat moss is composed of decayed vegetable and plant matter that works in conjunction with the cow manure and topsoil to give your plants a well-balanced medium in which to grow. The peat moss fluffs up, separates, and absorbs the moisture of the damp topsoil, and the manure acts as a natural, gentle fertilizer. Be sure not to use too much peat moss, as it can dry out the topsoil. Do not use too much manure, because even though it is organic and gentler than other chemically produced fertilizers, it can still burn the plants. **Burning** is a chemical reaction a plant experiences when it is over fertilized. The plant itself will give off the appearance of having been touched by too much heat, and in this instance, the appearance comes from the chemicals in the fertilizing material. Mixing a soil medium is sort of like putting a cake batter together. If you mix it properly, it makes up just the right concoction to feed your seeds just what they need to get off to a great start. Any good garden center should have several varieties and quantities of peat moss and both chicken and cow manure, along with different types of topsoil, available for purchase.

Whatever medium you decide to use, whether it is sphagnum moss, pure vermiculite, commercial potting mix, or potting mix of several materials that you have put together yourself, all that is really necessary for successful germination is good air circulation, moisture retention, and drainage. Because your seeds already have a nutrient store available, nutrients in the germination mixture are only important once the plant actually sprouts and begins to grow. The potting mixture will also need to be free from mold, disease, other plants or weeds, and insect infestation.

If you decide to incorporate actual garden dirt into your mixture, remember that you need to sterilize it before using, so that any soil borne diseases or insect life is irradiated. Heat kills bacteria, and there are several ways to do this. To sterilize soil, it can be either baked in the oven at a low temperature — 250 degrees — put in the microwave for ten minutes, or spread onto a plastic sheet and laid out in the full sun for at least one week with the hopes it does not rain. Because of the unpredictability of the weather, this last method should be a last resort. Keep in mind that if you decide to use vermiculite or moss or a mixture containing nothing but these two substances, you will need to feed the seedlings once they have sprouted, as neither of these contains any nutrient content. Most potting soil mixes contain a premeasured amount of plant food, but seedlings started in moss or vermiculite will require regular liquid feeding of a mild plant food solution of three parts water to one part fertilizer until they are ready to be transplanted into real soil.

Soil pH

Discussing pH levels in soil can be somewhat daunting, as each plant thrives in specific types better than others. Soil pH is the measurement of the soil acidity or alkalinity on a scale from 0 (acidic) to 14 (alkaline). Acidic soil has a pH below 7.0 (0 to 7.0), whereas alkaline soil has a pH larger than 7.0 (7.0 to 14). A level of 7.0 is considered neutral soil. Each plant, vegetable, fruit, and flower, has its own unique level at which it will grow best, just as humans have a preference as to their living conditions.

Testing your pH level

Testing your soil pH should be done often because certain conditions, such as adding fertilizers, can drastically change the pH level in your soil. This should not be a loathsome task, but a fun one that connects you with the beauty of nature and brings you satisfaction.

In order to test your soil pH level, you must have a device called a pH tester or meter. This device will measure the pH of your soil when inserted into the soil you intend to test. You can purchase a test kit for simple testing or a meter for continuous use. The following websites host kits and meters for both professional gardeners and beginners.

▸ Home Harvest Garden Supply **http://homeharvest.com/soiltesting.htm**

▸ Planet Natural

http://www.planetnatural.com/site/xdpy/sgc/Soil%20Care/Soil%20 pH%20&%20Test%20Kits

▸ Spectrum Technologies **www.specmeters.com/pH_Meters/**

▸ Nextag **www.nextag.com/soil-ph-meter/stores-html**

When considering whether to use a meter or a tester, take into account the size of your garden. Again, you want to enjoy testing your soil and watching your garden thrive.

What to do About Problems

Every time a farmer plants a particular crop in a field, he or she makes a bet that the crop will survive. Home gardeners do the same thing on a much smaller scale in their gardens. You plant what you think are healthy seeds and plants; work your magic with compost, plant food, proper watering, and basic tender, loving care; and then cross your fingers, take a deep breath, and wait for the best. Just like the farmer, you know that each season, after you have worked so hard at planning, planting, and then carefully nurturing your plants and seeds along to maturity, that inevitably, for whatever reasons, some of the resulting plants do much better than others. They were all planted at the same time, under the same conditions, and yet squash from two plants that are lying side by side in the same soil end up so different. For the purposes of selecting parent plants, ponder the mystery of how and why those two squash plants produced such vastly different vegetables.

There are many unknown contributing factors that will determine the actual results, but the biggest constant is the unpredictability of it all. Trying to figure out why some plants thrive and others do not is rather like doing detective work. There are clues to be discovered and puzzle pieces to be fitted together. The good news is that once the pieces of the puzzle can be put together, you can use what you have learned to predict future gardening scenarios.

Soil conditions, inclement weather, insects, disease, a lack of proper sunlight, and water requirements can all be contributing factors in the reasons that some plants thrive, and others do not. It is always a good idea to determine exactly why such losses occur and to note "how, why, and when." If you have not been keeping track of successes and failures in a journal or garden log, you might want to start now.

Pests and controlling them

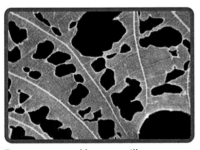

Damage caused by caterpillars

Because of the intrinsic nature of fruit trees, and the fact they are covered in luscious, edible fruit, they become a bigger target for garden pests than practically any other living plant. Think of it this way: the tree is composed of the trunk, which proves to be irresistible to deer and other gnawing, chewing animals. Then, the tree puts out leaves and blossoms, the favorite food for a host of caterpillars, cutting worms, and other assorted insects. Finally, the fruit itself arrives, and if the birds or the bats do not get it during its first stages of development, it becomes susceptible to any number of insect infestations and assaults. Before reaching for the pesticides, there are better and less harmful ways to protect your trees and their fruit from the marauding multitudes of unwanted garden pests.

As mentioned in the section on pollination, chemical pesticides can be harmful in many ways, not only to the bees that do the pollinating, but also to any other living thing that is exposed to them. As gardeners have become more environmentally conscious these days and strive to avoid deliberately doing anything to jeopardize the precarious balance between man and climate, they look for different ways to achieve the results they seek without harming their surroundings with toxic substances.

Chemicals that can infiltrate your food are never good under any circumstances, and if you use these pesticides in gardens, they are penetrating the air, soil, water, and the very food that you eventually consume. If you spray your trees with chemical pesticides, those harmful chemicals can contaminate the tree itself (which means that besides the pollinating bees, other useful insects will also be affected), the soil, and in turn, anything that comes into contact with it.

So, what are the alternatives? It is true that nature presents gardeners with the unwanted pests in the first place, but nature itself also furnishes gardeners with a multitude of ways to combat them. Just as there is a vast array of chemical pesticides you can use, there are many safe, organic ways to protect your trees without having to worry or feel guilty about the repercussions of using dangerous synthetics.

There are quite a few commercially prepared products on the market that are just as effective as chemical pesticides when it comes to controlling garden pests, but without the bad side effects. Go to PestWeb at **www.pestweb.com** for a comprehensive list of natural pesticides. Many common household items can be used in the garden for various purposes. Such things as garlic, horseradish, cayenne pepper, vinegar, onions, spearmint, chili peppers, and salt can be used in combinations and mixed into solutions to ward away insects and garden pests. Dish soap is an extremely effective organic pesticide and when placed around the perimeter of each tree, it will deter many types of destructive worms and bugs from crossing the dish detergent and climbing the bark. In the case of fruit trees, boric acid (available near the bandages at most pharmacies as it is commonly used as a medicine) can be sprinkled around the base to discourage certain types of fungus and molds.

Gardening in small spaces

Small gardens, which can range from a small patch of ground in a front, back, or courtyard to a porch, patio, or balcony, in which only container or planter gardening is possible, present unique challenges. For obvious reasons, those who must garden in these environments must be clever and inventive in choosing the types of plants from which to save seeds. If you decide that you want to include some fruit bushes or trees in your small garden, it would be wise to think about what you can plant that will be:

▸ A relatively decorative addition to the overall "look" of your garden

▸ Cost effective

▸ Easy to grow and maintain

This is not to say that you should feel prohibited by the size of your garden area. In so many ways, a small garden can give you hours of enjoyment and a great sense of satisfaction in the fruit, flowers, and vegetables that it delivers. By having a small garden, you will not have to spend time plowing and weeding, which is typically associated with the larger garden. When done creatively and using every bit of space available, the small garden can be just as lovely as the clever gardener can make it. Depending on the personality of the gardener, as well as the time and effort that he or she is willing to dedicate to the challenges gardening on a smaller scale presents, growing fruit in the small garden can prove to be very rewarding.

Feed and Fertilization

While your new crop of seedlings is making the transition from indoors to outdoors, they will need the same things that they needed when they were initially planted — the proper soil mixture, good light, appropriate watering, and a good fertilizer. There are any number of commercial products available, and every gardener you talk to will give you advice and opinions on what to use for the best possible outcome. Organic fertilizers are not as harsh as the chemically manufactured ones, and you can feel good that you are treating your plants to an environmentally friendly feeding program. You can make up your own compost tea or use watered down cow manure, but keep in mind that less is better. Until your seedlings have sprouted their first leaves, do not worry about fertilizing them because they will have been absorbing the nutrients that are stored within the planted seed itself.

When the seedlings have reached the stage where they need to be fertilized, use the same philosophy you use for watering for fertilizing: Too much of either can be detrimental to your plants. Instead of fertilizing too much at one time, spread out the feedings over a few days, and feed only the weakest solutions of whatever fertilizer you have chosen to use. You can tell if your plants need fertilizer by judging how they are progressing. As they gain strength and mature, you can increase the potency of the mixture. Start with the three parts water to one part fertilizer ratio, and feed only once or twice every two weeks.

Long-term Care

Once the last danger of frost is finally past, your plants will begin to establish themselves in their new homes in the garden and to grow and thrive. As they grow, they will begin to compete for space and nutrients. The bigger they get, the more crowded the garden becomes.

While the new seedlings are becoming healthy plants, they still need the same attention and care as they did while they were germinating and sprouting. Now that they are outside, you will want to observe how much water they are getting. If you are in a humid environment, you will likely not have to water your plants every day except in the hottest months of the year. If you are in a dry environment, like the desert or high plains regions of the United States, you will be watering more often. As a general rule of thumb, if the soil appears dry on the surface, do not rush to water. Instead, stick a finger down into the dirt. If it feels damp beneath the surface, you can probably go at least another day until the next watering. If it is dry beneath the surface (roughly 1/4 inch beneath the surface), it is time to water.

There are many things that gardeners can disagree about, including when, how, or if to fertilize plants. Some gardeners fertilize their plants on a regular basis and would never think of doing otherwise. Other gardeners only fertilize when they think their plants are performing as if they need it. They feel that fertilizing is not necessary if the soil medium has been sufficiently prepared and actually prefer their plants to adjust to and grow without adding artificial growth boosters of any kind. While your seedlings were becoming adult plants, they most assuredly needed fertilizing during various phases of their development.

Once they go outside and become part of the natural environment, the question of fertilizer becomes a personal choice. You can base your decision on the results you have achieved in previous gardening scenarios, and how your plants seem to be progressing in their new environment. If you make the decision to go ahead and fertilize your plants, countless brands of commercial fertilizers are available. Some of them are very specialized and should only be used on specific types of plants. Others are balanced mixtures that can be used in a more general application. Miracle-Gro and Osmocote by Scott are two nonorganic general plant foods that are very effective, and most growers, greenhouses, and home improvement stores offer these nonorganic mixtures, as well as an array of organic plant foods and insecticides. You can also mix up your own organic plant food out of equal parts of compost and cow manure. Just be sure to apply any fertilizer that you do decide upon sparingly, and do not use it too often as too much of it can harm your plants.

Watering or Drowning?

Of all the common mistakes most gardeners make, overwatering is the most prevalent. It is unfortunate that most people tend to think that water is the cure all for anything that ails a weak or wobbly plant. Why is it that whenever gardeners quickly and accurately diagnose the problem, their first solution is to grab the watering can? The truth is, most plants respond very well with less water than you think they want or need. Once the plants have matured to a height of 3 or 4 inches, you can ease off the misting process. As long as their root systems are adequately watered, the rest of the plant will be just fine. While your seedlings are gaining strength enough to be taken outdoors, pay close attention to how the soil around them feels to the touch and how heavy each flat or container feels when lifted. If the soil feels dry to the touch and the container is light when handled, it should be watered. If the soil feels damp and the flat is heavy when you pick it up, no water is necessary. Start watering by saturating the soil of each container, but not to the point that soil begins to float in the water. Let the water soak in, and do not water again until the surface of the soil feels dry to the touch.

After carefully watering as needed, make a daily inspection of the conditions of the soil, temperature, and light to make sure that nothing happens to jeopardize not only your own hard work in getting all the growing conditions just right, but also the plants themselves. Now is the time to check for any disease that might have manifested itself in the soil, or insect infestation that could have occurred. It sometimes seems that disease and insects can happen overnight; in reality, unless the conditions of the soil were sterile and perfect at the time of planting, it is common that one or two flats or containers might have somehow been contaminated. If you discover during your daily inspections that anything has infected the seeds or seedlings, dispose of the contaminated soil, seeds, or plants as any plant nearby could become infected.

As your seedlings sprout and grow, you will need to thin them in order for the best and strongest plants to get even more nutrients from the soil. While thinning is sometimes difficult for those who place a lot of value in every single plant, it must be done. Just as it is with too many people in one room, those little seedlings are competing for all of the air, light, and moisture that are available. In order for the fittest to survive, some weaker plants must be sacrificed. To thin the plants in your garden, instead of yanking the condemned plants up by their fragile roots, use small scissors to cut off the tops of the plants down to the soil. This way you are culling out the weakest specimens and yet not taking the chance of injuring the plants next to those that are being eliminated.

Architectural Elements, Arbors, and Other Supports for your Plants

As gardening has enjoyed a sort of renaissance in the last few years, more manufacturers have recognized that gardeners have become targets for promoting all types of merchandise to be used outdoors. All it takes is a trip to the mall or home improvement store or even to flip through some of the more well-known catalogs to know that you could spend thousands of dollars on wonderful garden accents of all kinds.

Of all the garden decorations that are out there, perhaps the most beautiful and functional are architectural elements. They can be enormous, dramatic structures made of wrought iron, copper, wood, or any number of other materials, or they might be as simple as a tall inverted cone shaped cage. In any event, either style would be a lovely way to support a grapevine you have planted in a large container.

Arbors are a popular attraction for adults as well as children. An **arbor** is usually any tall, arch-shaped structure constructed of metal or wood that provides support for any sort of trailing or vine-like plant. It may be used for grapes, morning glory, bougainvillea, or other varieties of vining plants that can be trained upon them. Climbing roses, for instance, look especially lovely growing on a decorative arbor. Besides being beautiful architectural features, the sight of any type of arbor laden with fragrant bunches of deep purple Concord grapes is awe inspiring to both the eye and the taste buds. While you may be more accustomed to seeing arbors covered in climbing flowering plants, such as clematis or climbing roses, arbors can serve the same purpose for grapevines as they do for those plants.

You can purchase a commercially constructed arbor at any garden center, or if you or someone you know is handy with a hammer and nails, you can put together a simple but sturdy arbor for a reasonable price. Arbors are particularly useful for grapes to increase their productivity. As with any fruit, grapes need as much sun as possible in order to thrive and to manufacture the sugars that make them taste so good. Therefore, you will want to find as sunny a place as possible to install your arbor. Follow these steps to help grow healthy vines.

▶ Place the arbor in the location that you have chosen, and make sure that it is anchored to your satisfaction.

▶ Plant the vines on either side in planters that will be able to accommodate the weight of the vines when they have reached full maturity.

▶ Because this arbor element will become such a decorative feature of your garden, you might want to choose planters that are more aesthetically pleasing than the usual plain terra cotta or resin pots that are available. Resin is a synthetic material that feels like plastic, but can be cleverly produced to resemble organic materials, such as terra cotta. Preconstructed wooden arbors that have large square planter tubs attached to either side of the structure itself are available, and these in particular, because of the volume of soil that they can contain, are perfect for growing grapes and vines with larger root systems.

If you do not have the room for an arbor-type frame for your vines, but you have plenty of sun on an outside wall and are willing to use some invasive hardware on the surface, you can train the vines to climb on any sturdy trellis that has been set into an adequately sized container. A **trellis** is any flat, one-dimensional structure made of metal, wood, or other material that can be used as a brace on which to train plants. After filling the planter with soil medium, push it flush up against the wall, and sink the trellis down as far as it will go. Using the proper anchoring hardware for your surface material (brick or wood), attach the trellis to the wall. Grapevines, particularly, are some of the longest living plants, as any visit to a well-established vineyard will attest. They can survive and produce fruit for years, and as the grapevines mature they thicken, and then when they begin to bear fruit, the grapes cause the vines to be heavy. Anchoring the trellis to the wall prevents the vines from pulling the entire structure down onto the ground. Depending on how long the containers are that you are using, plant one to two vines in the container and — as the vines grow — tie them up onto the trellis, using noninvasive materials, such as strips of soft cloth or cording that will not cut into the surface of the vine. Some gardeners swear by sections of old panty hose for this purpose. The panty hose is soft and pliable and will not harm the surface of the growing vines.

CONCLUSION:

Get Out There and Save Seeds

Saving seeds is such a uniquely rewarding experience. You become a grandparent of sorts when you nurture a plant along to the point it produces seed, and then take those seeds, carefully preserving them for future growth. When the plants you get from the store or a pack of seeds give you seeds and plants of your own, it is like they truly become yours. You nurtured a creation from idea to reality, from seed to seed.

Planning your garden, applying all the knowledge you have of the plants you love, and getting them to return year after year is a creative, thoughtful, fulfilling process. Take some time to plan it out and plan some time to enjoy your garden as well.

Planning Your Garden

Some of you are lucky enough to have access to large areas of open space you can plow and rake into organized rows of vegetables, fruits, and flowers, while the rest of you live in more urban areas and must choose to garden on a smaller scale, using more enterprising methods to maximize the space you have available. Do not feel suppressed by a lack of room; this just means that you need to consider other planting options, perhaps implementing raised beds and container planters.

While planning a garden is certainly a pleasant way to pass the time, keep in mind some basic rules that will help guide you to achieving optimal harvests and eliminate any worries you have about possible obstacles you may face. First, you must ask yourself some preliminary questions:

▶ How much time am I willing and able to dedicate to the work involved in maintaining the garden?

▶ Am I aware of and capable of the actual physical work?

▶ How much money will it take, and am I willing to spend it?

▶ Where is the best place for a garden? How big does it need to be?

▶ What do I do if I do not have a lot of room?

Once you know all of these answers, consider:

▶ How much beauty can I tolerate in my garden?

▶ Do I know how lovely the flowers will smell?

▶ Will I ever be able to eat fruit from a grocery store again, or will I be spoiled?

▶ Can I really enjoy being productive, saving money, and eating healthy?

▶ Will my family forgive me for spending so much time away from them?

Surely, there is work involved, but the enjoyment is many times over a reward for the hard work you put into your garden. Enjoy it. Cherish it. Take all of your wonderful ideas and aspirations for your garden, make a formal plan, and put it to action.

Your Garden Will Never be the Same Again

When you have your new seeds, and you are ready to fill in all the gaps you have had in your garden for years, pause for a minute. Look at your garden as it is. All the empty corners — filled. All the older plants — revived. All the beauty you imagine — on the horizon. The seeds you have in your hand are about to change your garden in ways you had only imagined before. Because expense will no longer be an issue, your garden will be lush, full, and beautiful. It truly will take on a new life and a new shape. The work you put into saving your seeds will make your garden shine. It will never be the same again.

You Will Never be the Same Again

The amount of fulfillment you will experience will bring you great joy. It is one thing to put a plant someone else started into the ground. It is a rewarding experience of an entirely different kind when you start a new plant from seeds you harvested. It is like the difference a family cook experiences when opening a can of soup. It is good, yes. It works, yes. People are satiated by soup. But the level of fulfillment is much higher when an adoring family cherishes the special dish the cook lovingly prepares from a long-held family recipe. When an artist paints an original oil painting, the value is many times that of the poster made from it. The plant from the garden center is the poster, not unique and not the work of the artist's hand. The plant from the seed you harvested will be your masterpiece. You and your garden will never be the same again.

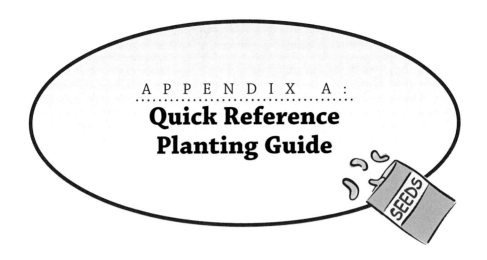

Quick Reference Planting Guide

Each plant referenced in the vegetables, fruits, and flowers chapters of this text has recommendations for where it is likely to grow successfully. The following is a quick reference for which zones the plants discussed will grow in, by zone. Locate your zone on the map below, and then reference the chart to see what you can grow in your zone and save seeds from.

Northern/Cooler Zones

Plants, Alphabetically	1	2a	2b	3a	3b	4a	4b	5a	5b	6a	6b
Almond								✖	✖	✖	✖
Alyssum				✖	✖	✖	✖	✖	✖	✖	✖
Amaranth	✖	✖	✖	✖	✖	✖	✖	✖	✖	✖	✖
Apricot						✖	✖	✖	✖	✖	✖
Aster				✖	✖	✖	✖	✖	✖	✖	✖
Astilbe				✖	✖	✖	✖	✖	✖	✖	✖
Baby's breath				✖	✖	✖	✖	✖	✖	✖	✖
Bachelor's button				✖	✖	✖	✖	✖	✖	✖	✖
Basil	✖	✖	✖	✖	✖	✖	✖	✖	✖	✖	✖
Bee balm						✖	✖	✖	✖	✖	✖
Beets	✖	✖	✖	✖	✖	✖	✖	✖	✖	✖	✖

Plants, Alphabetically	1	2a	2b	3a	3b	4a	4b	5a	5b	6a	6b
Bellflower				✖	✖	✖	✖	✖	✖	✖	✖
Blackberries								✖	✖	✖	✖
Black-eyed Susan				✖	✖	✖	✖	✖	✖	✖	✖
Blueberries				✖	✖	✖	✖	✖	✖	✖	✖
Borage or starflower	✖	✖	✖	✖	✖	✖	✖	✖	✖	✖	✖
Broccoli				✖	✖	✖	✖	✖	✖	✖	✖
Brussels sprouts						✖	✖	✖	✖	✖	✖
Cabbage	✖	✖	✖	✖	✖	✖	✖	✖	✖	✖	✖
Calendula		✖	✖	✖	✖	✖	✖	✖	✖	✖	✖
Cantaloupe				✖	✖	✖	✖	✖	✖	✖	✖
Canterbury bells								✖	✖	✖	✖
Carrot	✖	✖	✖	✖	✖	✖	✖	✖	✖	✖	✖
Catnip				✖	✖	✖	✖	✖	✖	✖	✖
Cauliflower				✖	✖	✖	✖	✖	✖	✖	✖
Celeriac				✖	✖	✖	✖	✖	✖	✖	✖
Celery				✖	✖	✖	✖	✖	✖	✖	✖
Celtuce				✖	✖	✖	✖	✖	✖	✖	✖
Chickory	✖	✖	✖	✖	✖	✖	✖	✖	✖	✖	✖
Chinese cabbage	✖	✖	✖	✖	✖	✖	✖	✖	✖	✖	✖
Chives				✖	✖	✖	✖	✖	✖	✖	✖
Chrysanthemum, or mums				✖	✖	✖	✖	✖	✖	✖	✖
Cilantro										✖	✖
Clematis				✖	✖	✖	✖	✖	✖	✖	✖
Columbine				✖	✖	✖	✖	✖	✖	✖	✖
Common bean	✖	✖	✖	✖	✖	✖	✖	✖	✖	✖	✖
Common onions				✖	✖	✖	✖	✖	✖	✖	✖
Coneflower				✖	✖	✖	✖	✖	✖	✖	✖
Coreopsis						✖	✖	✖	✖	✖	✖
Corn				✖	✖	✖	✖	✖	✖	✖	✖
Cosmos								✖	✖	✖	✖
Cranberries				✖	✖	✖	✖	✖	✖	✖	✖
Cucumber				✖	✖	✖	✖	✖	✖	✖	✖
Dill				✖	✖	✖	✖	✖	✖	✖	✖
Eggplant									✖	✖	✖
Fava bean				✖	✖	✖	✖	✖	✖	✖	✖
Fennel						✖	✖	✖	✖	✖	✖

Plants, Alphabetically	1	2a	2b	3a	3b	4a	4b	5a	5b	6a	6b
Flax						✖	✖	✖	✖	✖	✖
Forget-me-not						✖	✖	✖	✖	✖	✖
Gaillardia				✖	✖	✖	✖	✖	✖	✖	✖
Garden pea		✖	✖	✖	✖	✖	✖	✖	✖	✖	✖
Garlic				✖	✖	✖	✖	✖	✖	✖	✖
Grapes				✖	✖	✖	✖	✖	✖	✖	✖
Hollyhock		✖	✖	✖	✖	✖	✖	✖	✖	✖	✖
Honeydew				✖	✖	✖	✖	✖	✖	✖	✖
Huckleberries				✖	✖	✖	✖	✖	✖	✖	✖
Jerusalem artichoke				✖	✖	✖	✖	✖	✖	✖	✖
Kale		✖	✖	✖	✖	✖	✖	✖	✖	✖	✖
Larkspur				✖	✖	✖	✖	✖	✖	✖	✖
Lavender hyssop						✖	✖	✖	✖	✖	✖
Leeks		✖	✖	✖	✖	✖	✖	✖	✖	✖	✖
Lettuce						✖	✖	✖	✖	✖	✖
Lilacs		✖	✖	✖	✖	✖	✖	✖	✖	✖	✖
Lima bean				✖	✖	✖	✖	✖	✖	✖	✖
Lobelia						✖	✖	✖	✖	✖	✖
Lupine						✖	✖	✖	✖	✖	✖
Mallow, rose						✖	✖	✖	✖	✖	✖
Mango melon		✖	✖	✖	✖	✖	✖	✖	✖	✖	✖
Marigold		✖	✖	✖	✖	✖	✖	✖	✖	✖	✖
Morning glory						✖	✖	✖	✖	✖	✖
Muskmelon		✖	✖	✖	✖	✖	✖	✖	✖	✖	✖
Nasturtium						✖	✖	✖	✖	✖	✖
Nectarine								✖	✖	✖	✖
Pansy		✖	✖	✖	✖	✖	✖	✖	✖	✖	✖
Parsley		✖	✖	✖	✖	✖	✖	✖	✖	✖	✖
Parsnip				✖	✖	✖	✖	✖	✖	✖	✖
Peach								✖	✖	✖	✖
Peppers				✖	✖	✖	✖	✖	✖	✖	✖
Petunia				✖	✖	✖	✖	✖	✖	✖	✖
Phlox				✖	✖	✖	✖	✖	✖	✖	✖
Plum						✖	✖	✖	✖	✖	✖
Pocket melon				✖	✖	✖	✖	✖	✖	✖	✖
Poppy		✖	✖	✖	✖	✖	✖	✖	✖	✖	✖

Plants, Alphabetically	1	2a	2b	3a	3b	4a	4b	5a	5b	6a	6b
Potatoes				✖	✖	✖	✖	✖	✖	✖	✖
Primrose		✖	✖	✖	✖	✖	✖	✖	✖	✖	✖
Quinoa				✖	✖	✖	✖	✖	✖	✖	✖
Radish		✖	✖	✖	✖	✖	✖	✖	✖	✖	✖
Raspberries				✖	✖	✖	✖	✖	✖	✖	✖
Rocambole				✖	✖	✖	✖	✖	✖	✖	✖
Rutabaga				✖	✖	✖	✖	✖	✖	✖	✖
Sage, culinary varieties								✖	✖	✖	✖
Salsify										✖	✖
Salvia				✖	✖	✖	✖	✖	✖	✖	✖
Snake melon				✖	✖	✖	✖	✖	✖	✖	✖
Snapdragon						✖	✖	✖	✖	✖	✖
Sour cherry				✖	✖	✖	✖	✖	✖	✖	✖
Spinach				✖	✖	✖	✖	✖	✖	✖	✖
Squashes		✖	✖	✖	✖	✖	✖	✖	✖	✖	✖
Strawberries		✖	✖	✖	✖	✖	✖	✖	✖	✖	✖
Sunflowers								✖	✖	✖	✖
Sweet pea	✖	✖	✖	✖	✖	✖	✖	✖	✖	✖	✖
Thimbleberries				✖	✖	✖	✖	✖	✖	✖	✖
Tomatoes	✖	✖	✖	✖	✖	✖	✖	✖	✖	✖	✖
Turnip				✖	✖	✖	✖	✖	✖	✖	✖
Verbena		✖	✖	✖	✖	✖	✖	✖	✖	✖	✖
Watermelon				✖	✖	✖	✖	✖	✖	✖	✖
Yard long bean				✖	✖	✖	✖	✖	✖	✖	✖
Zinnia						✖	✖	✖	✖	✖	✖

Southern/Warmer Zones

Plants, Alphabetically	7a	7b	8a	8b	9a	9b	10a	10b	11
Ageratum			✖	✖	✖	✖	✖	✖	✖
Almond	✖	✖	✖	✖					
Alyssum	✖	✖	✖	✖	✖	✖	✖	✖	
Amaranth	✖	✖	✖	✖	✖	✖	✖	✖	✖
Apricot	✖	✖	✖	✖	✖				
Armenian cucumber	✖	✖	✖	✖	✖	✖	✖	✖	✖

	1	2	3	4	5	6	7	8	9
Artichoke	✖	✖	✖	✖	✖	✖	✖	✖	✖
Aster	✖	✖	✖	✖					
Astilbe	✖	✖	✖	✖					
Baby's breath	✖	✖	✖	✖	✖	✖			
Bachelor's button	✖	✖	✖	✖	✖	✖	✖	✖	
Basil	✖	✖	✖	✖	✖	✖	✖	✖	✖
Bee balm	✖	✖	✖	✖	✖	✖			
Beets	✖	✖	✖	✖	✖	✖	✖	✖	✖
Bellflower	✖	✖	✖	✖					
Blackberries	✖	✖	✖	✖					
Black-eyed Susan	✖	✖	✖	✖	✖	✖			
Blueberries	✖	✖	✖	✖					
Borage or starflower	✖	✖	✖	✖	✖	✖	✖	✖	✖
Broccoli	✖	✖	✖	✖	✖	✖	✖	✖	
Brussels sprouts	✖	✖	✖	✖					
Cabbage	✖	✖	✖	✖	✖	✖	✖	✖	✖
Calendula	✖	✖	✖	✖	✖	✖			
Cantaloupe	✖	✖	✖	✖	✖	✖			
Canterbury bells	✖	✖	✖	✖	✖	✖			
Carrot	✖	✖	✖	✖	✖	✖	✖	✖	✖
Catnip	✖	✖	✖	✖	✖	✖			
Cauliflower	✖	✖	✖	✖	✖	✖			
Celeriac	✖	✖	✖	✖	✖	✖			
Celery	✖	✖	✖	✖	✖	✖			
Celosia							✖	✖	✖
Celtuce	✖	✖	✖	✖	✖	✖	✖	✖	✖
Chayote	✖	✖	✖	✖	✖	✖	✖	✖	✖
Chick pea	✖	✖	✖	✖	✖	✖	✖	✖	✖
Chickory	✖	✖	✖	✖	✖	✖	✖	✖	✖
Chinese cabbage	✖	✖	✖	✖	✖	✖	✖	✖	✖
Chinese lantern			✖	✖	✖	✖	✖	✖	
Chives	✖	✖							
Chrysanthemum, or mums	✖	✖	✖	✖	✖	✖			
Cilantro	✖	✖	✖	✖	✖	✖	✖	✖	✖
Clematis	✖	✖	✖	✖	✖	✖			
Collard greens			✖	✖	✖	✖	✖	✖	✖
Columbine	✖	✖	✖	✖	✖	✖			

Common bean	✖	✖	✖	✖	✖	✖	✖	✖	✖
Common onions	✖	✖	✖	✖	✖	✖			
Coneflower	✖	✖	✖	✖					
Coreopsis	✖	✖	✖	✖	✖	✖			
Corn	✖	✖	✖	✖	✖	✖	✖	✖	
Cosmos	✖	✖	✖	✖	✖	✖	✖	✖	
Cowpea					✖	✖	✖	✖	✖
Cranberries	✖	✖							
Cucumber	✖	✖	✖	✖	✖	✖	✖	✖	✖
Daisy			✖	✖	✖	✖	✖	✖	✖
Dill	✖	✖	✖	✖	✖	✖	✖	✖	✖
Eggplant	✖	✖	✖	✖	✖	✖	✖	✖	✖
Fava bean	✖	✖	✖	✖	✖	✖	✖	✖	✖
Fennel	✖	✖	✖	✖	✖	✖	✖	✖	
Flax	✖	✖	✖	✖	✖	✖			
Forget-me-not	✖	✖	✖	✖	✖	✖			
Four-o'clock			✖	✖	✖	✖	✖	✖	✖
Gaillardia	✖	✖	✖	✖	✖	✖	✖	✖	
Garden pea	✖	✖	✖	✖	✖	✖	✖	✖	
Gourds	✖	✖	✖	✖	✖	✖	✖	✖	✖
Grapes	✖	✖	✖	✖	✖	✖	✖	✖	
Hollyhock	✖	✖	✖	✖	✖	✖	✖	✖	
Honeydew	✖	✖	✖	✖	✖	✖	✖	✖	
Huckleberries	✖	✖	✖	✖	✖	✖			
Jerusalem artichoke	✖	✖	✖	✖	✖	✖			
Kale	✖	✖	✖	✖	✖	✖	✖	✖	
Larkspur	✖	✖	✖	✖	✖	✖			
Lavender hyssop	✖	✖	✖	✖	✖	✖	✖	✖	
Leeks	✖	✖	✖	✖					
Lettuce	✖	✖	✖	✖	✖	✖			
Lilacs	✖	✖							
Lima bean	✖	✖	✖	✖	✖	✖	✖	✖	
Lobelia	✖	✖	✖	✖	✖	✖	✖	✖	✖
Luffa	✖	✖	✖	✖	✖	✖	✖	✖	✖
Lupine	✖	✖	✖	✖					
Mallow, rose	✖	✖	✖	✖	✖	✖			
Mango melon	✖	✖	✖	✖	✖	✖			

Marigold	✖	✖	✖	✖	✖	✖	✖	✖	✖
Morning glory	✖	✖	✖	✖	✖	✖	✖	✖	✖
Muskmelon	✖	✖	✖	✖	✖	✖			
Nasturtium	✖	✖	✖	✖	✖	✖	✖	✖	✖
Nectarine	✖	✖	✖	✖	✖	✖			
Painted tongue					✖	✖	✖	✖	✖
Pansy	✖	✖	✖	✖					
Parsley	✖	✖	✖	✖	✖	✖	✖		
Parsnip	✖	✖	✖	✖	✖	✖			
Peach	✖	✖	✖	✖	✖	✖			
Peanut				✖	✖	✖	✖	✖	✖
Peppers	✖	✖	✖	✖	✖	✖	✖	✖	✖
Petunia	✖	✖	✖	✖	✖	✖	✖	✖	✖
Phlox	✖	✖	✖	✖	✖	✖			
Pigeon pea					✖	✖	✖	✖	✖
Plum	✖	✖	✖	✖	✖	✖	✖	✖	
Pocket melon	✖	✖	✖	✖	✖	✖			
Poppy	✖	✖	✖	✖	✖	✖	✖	✖	
Potatoes	✖	✖	✖	✖	✖	✖	✖	✖	✖
Primrose	✖	✖	✖	✖	✖	✖	✖	✖	
Quinoa	✖	✖	✖	✖	✖	✖	✖	✖	✖
Radish	✖	✖							
Raspberries	✖	✖	✖	✖					
Runner bean	✖	✖	✖	✖	✖	✖	✖	✖	✖
Rutabaga	✖	✖	✖	✖	✖	✖	✖		
Sage, culinary varieties	✖	✖	✖	✖	✖	✖	✖	✖	
Salsify	✖	✖	✖	✖	✖	✖	✖	✖	
Salvia	✖	✖	✖	✖					
Snake melon	✖	✖	✖	✖	✖	✖			
Snapdragon	✖	✖	✖	✖	✖	✖	✖	✖	✖
Sour cherry	✖	✖	✖	✖					
Soybean	✖	✖	✖	✖	✖	✖			
Spinach	✖	✖	✖	✖	✖	✖			
Squashes	✖	✖	✖	✖	✖	✖			
Strawberries	✖	✖	✖	✖	✖	✖	✖	✖	✖
Sunflowers	✖	✖	✖	✖	✖	✖			
Sweet pea	✖	✖	✖	✖	✖	✖	✖	✖	✖

Tepary bean	✖	✖	✖	✖	✖	✖	✖	✖	
Thimbleberries	✖	✖	✖	✖	✖	✖			
Tobacco or nicotiana					✖	✖	✖	✖	✖
Tomatillo	✖	✖	✖	✖	✖	✖	✖	✖	✖
Tomatoes	✖	✖	✖	✖	✖	✖	✖	✖	✖
Turnip	✖	✖	✖	✖	✖	✖	✖	✖	
Verbena	✖	✖	✖	✖	✖	✖	✖	✖	✖
Watermelon	✖	✖	✖	✖	✖	✖	✖	✖	✖
Yard long bean	✖	✖	✖	✖	✖	✖			
Zinnia	✖	✖	✖	✖	✖	✖	✖	✖	✖

APPENDIX B :

Seed Exchanges and Cooperatives

Seed Savers Exchange

Founded in 1975, this nonprofit, 80-acre multigenerational family farm in Iowa boasts of passing on more than 1 million seed samples of heirloom plants to gardeners. **www.seedsavers.org**

Tribe.net Seed Exchange

Tribe.net is an online community consisting of many different forums. Their seed exchange is long running and active with more than 1,000 hobbyist gardeners. **http://seedexchange.tribe.net/**

Garden Web Seed Exchange

An online forum, here gardeners post requests for seeds they want and offer up those they have available to share with other gardeners. **http://forums2.gardenweb.com/forums/exseed/**

Seed Swaps Seed Traders

Seed Swaps is a free, online forum that connects gardeners interested in swapping seeds. **www.seedswaps.com**

Southern Seed Legacy Project

Based at the University of Georgia, this endeavor centers around the preservation of seeds from the southeastern quarter of the country. **www.uga.edu/ebl/ssl/**

Appalachian Heirloom Seed Conservatory

This Kentucky-based conservatory has a small, but growing inventory of heirloom varieties that thrive in the Appalachian region. P.O. Box 915, Richmond, KY 40476

Maine Seed Saving Network

This New England-region society hosts annual seed swaps among its members each spring. P.O. Box 126, Penobscot, ME 04476

Garden State Heirloom Seed Society

This nonprofit, New Jersey-based membership organization involves gardeners, farmers, and individuals in plant vocations and works on many fronts to preserve historical gardening practices, including heirloom seed saving. **www.historyyoucaneat.org**

The American Horticultural Society

The American Horticultural Society is one of the oldest national gardening organizations and offers education for gardeners at all levels. **www.ahs.org**

Herb Society of America

The Herb Society of America offers a variety of publication and education programs, and also offers networking and education opportunities. **www.herbsociety.org**

National Gardening Association

The National Gardening Association boasts the largest variety of gardening content for educators and consumers, ranging from publications to lesson plans to general information. **www.garden.org**

APPENDIX C:
Mail Order Sources for Seeds

Alberta Nurseries Bow Seeds
www.gardenersweb.ca

Applewood Seed Company
www.applewoodseed.com

Arrowhead Alpines
www.arrowhead-alpines.com

The Banana Tree, Inc.
www.banana-tree.com

Blazing Star Nursery
www.blazing-star.com

Bluestem Prairie Nursery
www.bluestemnursery.com

Bowman's Hill Wildflower Preserve
www.bhwp.org

Burgess Seed and Plant Co.
www.eburgess.com

The Chas. C. Hart Seed Co.
www.hartseed.com

Clyde Robin Seed Co.
www.clyderobin.com

Comstock Garden Seeds
www.comstockferre.com

The Cook's Garden
www.cooksgarden.com

Eagle Creek Seed Potatoes
www.seedpotatoes.ca

Easyliving Natural Perennial
Wildflowers
www.easywildflowers.com

F.W. Schumacher Co., Inc.
www.treeshrubseeds.com

Farmer Seed and Nursery
www.farmerseed.com

Ferry-Morse Seeds
www.ferry-morse.com

Four Seasons Nursery
www.4seasonsnurseries.com

Garden of Edith Nursery
www.garden-of-edith.com

Gardens North
www.gardensnorth.com

Girard Nurseries
www.girardnurseries.com

Gurney's Seed & Nursery Co.
www.gurneys.com

Harris Seeds
www.harrisseeds.com

Henry Fields Seed & Nursery Co.
www.henryfields.com

Hobbs & Hopkins, Ltd.
www.protimelawnseed.com

Holland Wildflower Farm
www.hwildflower.com

J.W. Jung Seed Co.
www.jungseed.com

Johnny's Selected Seeds
www.johnnyseeds.com

Johnston Seed Company
www.johnstonseed.com

Kettleby Herb Farms
www.kettlebyherbfarms.com

Kitazawa Seed Co.
www.kitazawaseed.com

Larner Seeds
www.larnerseeds.com

Local Harvest
www.localharvest.org

Michigan Wildflower Farm
www.michiganwildflowerfarm.com

Native Gardens
www.native-gardens.com

Native Plant Nursery
www.jfnew.com

Native Sons
www.nativeson.com

The Natural Gardening Company
www.naturalgardening.com

Nichols Garden Nursery
www.nicholsgardennursery.com

Organica Seed
www.organicaseed.com

Park Seed Co., Inc.
www.parkseed.com

Pinetree Garden Seeds
www.superseeds.com

Plants of the Southwest
www.plantsofthesouthwest.com

Prairie Moon Nursery
www.prairiemoon.com

Prairie Nursery
www.prairienursery.com

R.H. Shumway's
www.rhshumway.com

Redwood City Seed Company
www.ecoseeds.com

Renee's Garden Seeds
www.reneesgarden.com

Richters Herb Specialists
www.richters.com

The Rosemary House and Gardens
www.therosemaryhouse.com

S & S Seeds
www.ssseeds.com

Sandy Mush Herb Nursery
www.sandymushherbs.com

Seeds of Distinction
www.seedsofdistinction.com

Seeds Trust
www.seedstrust.com

Select Seeds
www.selectseeds.com

Sharp Brothers Seed Co.
www.buffalobrandseed.com

Stock Seed Farms, Inc.
www.stockseed.com

Stokes Seeds
www.stokeseeds.com

Territorial Seed Company
www.territorial-seed.com

Theodore Payne Foundation
www.theodorepayne.org

Thompson & Morgan, Ltd.
www.thompson-morgan.com

Tomato Growers Supply Co.
www.tomatogrowers.com

TwilleySeed
www.twilleyseed.com

Vermont Bean Seed Company
www.vermontbean.com

The Vermont Wildflower Farm
www.vermontwildflowerfarm.com

Veseys
www.veseys.com

Virtual Seeds
www.virtualseeds.com

W. Atlee Burpee & Co.
www.burpee.com

Well-Sweep Herb Farm
www.wellsweep.com

The Wildflower Seed & Tool
Company
www.wildflower-seed.com

Wildseed Farms, Inc.
www.wildseedfarms.com

William Dam Seeds
www.damseeds.com

Wind River Seed, Inc.
www.windriverseed.com

Wyatt-Quarles Seed Company
www.wqseeds.com

Yerba Buena Nursery
www.yerbabuenanursery.com

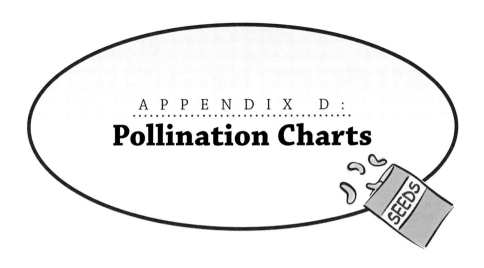

APPENDIX D:

Pollination Charts

Apple Pollination Information

The following chart shows which varieties of apples should not pollinate each other, and which varieties cannot pollinate with each other.

Apple Varieties ▲ Should not pollinate (poor results) ✖ Cannot pollinate (not suitable)	Lodi	Pristine	Empire	Honeycrisp	Liberty	Jonafree	Jonathan	Gala	Golden Delicious	Jonagold	Red Delicious	Winter Banana	Crispin	Granny Smith	Winesap	Braeburn	Enterprise	Fuji	Arkansas Black	Red York	Gold Rush	Rome Beauty
Lodi	▲																		✖	✖	✖	✖
Pristine		▲																				
Empire			▲																			
Honeycrisp				▲															✖	✖	✖	
Liberty					▲																	
Jonafree						▲																
Jonathan							▲															
Gala								▲														
Golden Delicious									▲													
Jonagold	✖	✖	✖	✖	✖	✖	✖	✖	✖	✖	✖	✖	✖	✖	✖	✖	✖	✖	✖	✖	✖	
Red Delicious											▲											
Winter Banana												▲										
Crispin	✖	✖	✖	✖	✖	✖	✖	✖	✖	✖	✖	✖	✖	✖	✖	✖	✖	✖	✖	✖	✖	✖
Granny Smith														▲								
Winesap	✖	✖	✖	✖	✖	✖	✖	✖	✖	✖	✖	✖	✖	✖	✖	✖	✖	✖	✖	✖	✖	✖
Braeburn																▲						
Enterprise																	▲					
Fuji																		▲				
Arkansas Black	✖																		▲			
Red York	✖			✖																▲		
Gold Rush				✖																	▲	
Rome Beauty	✖			✖																		▲

Apple Bloom Compatibility Chart

The following chart displays the compatible bloom periods for certain varieties of apples.

Variety	Early Bloom						Midseason Bloom								Late Bloom			
Idared	◆	◆	◆	◆	◆	◆	◆	◆	◆	◆	◆	◆						
Manchurian (crabapple)	◆	◆	◆	◆	◆	◆	◆	◆	◆	◆	◆	◆						
Empire		◆	◆	◆	◆	◆	◆	◆	◆	◆	◆	◆	◆	◆				
Honeycrisp		◆	◆	◆	◆	◆	◆	◆	◆	◆	◆	◆	◆	◆				
Liberty		◆	◆	◆	◆	◆	◆	◆	◆	◆	◆	◆	◆					
Akane			◆	◆	◆	◆	◆	◆	◆	◆	◆	◆	◆	◆				
Jonafree			◆	◆	◆	◆	◆	◆	◆	◆	◆	◆	◆					
Jonathan			◆	◆	◆	◆	◆	◆	◆	◆	◆	◆	◆	◆	◆			
Redtree			◆	◆	◆	◆	◆	◆	◆	◆	◆	◆	◆	◆	◆			
Gala					◆	◆	◆	◆	◆	◆	◆	◆	◆	◆	◆	◆		
Golden Delicious					◆	◆	◆	◆	◆	◆	◆	◆	◆	◆	◆	◆		
Jonagold					◆	◆	◆	◆	◆	◆	◆	◆	◆	◆	◆	◆		
Red Delicious					◆	◆	◆	◆	◆	◆	◆	◆	◆	◆	◆	◆		
Winter Banana					◆	◆	◆	◆	◆	◆	◆	◆	◆	◆	◆	◆		
Crispin						◆	◆	◆	◆	◆	◆	◆	◆	◆	◆	◆	◆	◆
Granny Smith						◆	◆	◆	◆	◆	◆	◆	◆	◆	◆	◆	◆	◆
Snowdrift (crabapple)						◆	◆	◆	◆	◆	◆	◆	◆	◆	◆	◆	◆	◆
Braeburn							◆	◆	◆	◆	◆	◆	◆	◆	◆	◆	◆	◆
Enterprise							◆	◆	◆	◆	◆	◆	◆	◆	◆	◆	◆	◆
Fuji							◆	◆	◆	◆	◆	◆	◆	◆	◆	◆	◆	◆
Pristine							◆	◆	◆	◆	◆	◆	◆	◆	◆	◆	◆	◆
York							◆	◆	◆	◆	◆	◆	◆	◆	◆	◆	◆	◆
Gold Rush								◆	◆	◆	◆	◆	◆	◆	◆	◆	◆	◆
Rome								◆	◆	◆	◆	◆	◆	◆	◆	◆	◆	◆

Sweet Cherry Pollination Chart

In the following chart are some common varieties of sweet cherry. The list across the top includes the varieties to be pollinated. The highlighted cells below each variety indicate cultivars that are not suitable or will not pollinate them. Other varieties are considered good pollinators.

Sweet Cherry Varieties ◆ Can, but should not pollinate (poor results) ✖ Cannot pollinate (not suitable)	Black Tartarian	Royal Ann	Ranier	Van	Bing	Hardy Giant	Black Republican	Stella	Hedelfingen	Royalton	Lambert	Lapins	Gold	Sweetheart
Black Tartarian	✖													
Royal Ann		✖			✖						✖			
Ranier			✖											
Van				✖										
Bing					✖						✖			
Hardy Giant						✖								
Black Republican							✖							
Stella								▲						
Hedelfingen									✖					
Royalton										✖				
Lambert		✖			✖						✖			
Lapins												▲		
Gold													✖	
Sweetheart														✖

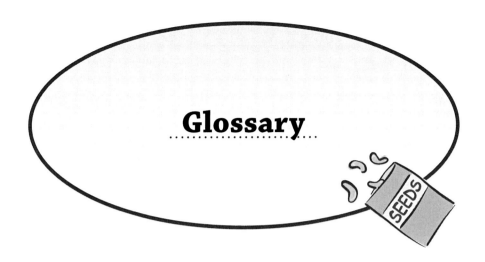

Glossary

abiotic pollination: pollination that occurs because of wind or water

albuminous: a seed with an endosperm

alternate-day caging: a form of mechanical isolation that uses two to four cages to cover similar, easily cross-pollinated plants. The gardener removes the cage from one variety of plant each day and covers it again at night.

anemochory: seed dispersal that happens by wind

angiosperms: flowering plants where seeds are produced inside a hard or fleshy structure, or fruit

arbor: any tall, arch-shaped structure constructed of metal or wood that provides support for any sort of trailing or vine-like plant

arils: fruit-like structures that are not actually fruit

autogamy: a plant's ability to fertilize itself

bagging: a method of isolating single plants by covering the flowers of the plant in a breathable fabric like spun polyester or muslin

biotic pollination: pollination that happens because of insects or animals

biparental inbreeding: when plants from the same ancestral line pollinate each other

blending: processing wet, slimy, or slick seed that grows into fleshy fruits

bolt to seed: The plant seeds earlier than is normal or desired for optimal harvesting.

burning: a chemical reaction that a plant experiences when it is over fertilized

caging: a means of mechanical isolation where plants are grown in wooden frames with screens or other breathable material covering the frame

calyptra: a membrane that covers a flower before it opens

cloche: small structures made of glass or clear plastic that are placed over cold-sensitive plants in winter

cold frame: a box with glass or clear plastic sides and a cover that protects plants from cold

corolla: the collective petals of the plant

cotyledons: seed leaves

cross-pollination: pollination of two distinct parent plants

cryogenics: preserving seeds using low temperatures; usually only attainable in a lab setting

depression: when the genetic condition of plants that inbreed deteriorate after several successive generations

dicotyledon (dicot) seed: a seed with two seed leaves

dioecious plants: plants that are singularly male or female and must rely on each other for reproduction

double fertilization: the joining of a single female embryo sac with two male sperm

elaiosomes: seed appendages that are primarily fat and protein

emasculation: removing the calyptra before the stigma is receptive to prevent self-pollination

endosperm: tissue that contains the nutrients and that is produced about the time of fertilization in angiosperms

epicotyl: the upper part of the seed's embryonic stem

epigeal: a plant that develops above ground

espalier: an ancient horticultural and agricultural practice of pruning and training the woody growth of plants to grow flat or straight, such as against a wall or on a trellis

exalbuminous: a seed without an endosperm

fanning: slowly pouring already threshed seeds that need further cleaning in front of a fan and allowing the heavy seeds to fall while the plant debris blows far away

fermenting: soaking the seeds and the plant flesh that surrounds the seeds for a couple days; this also helps rid the seeds of certain diseases

flat: the shallow, rectangular plastic tray that holds starter plants or plant bands

grafting: artificially attaching a cut portion of a plant onto a parent of the same species

green harvesting: harvesting seeds earlier than normal

greengrocers: retailers that specialize in selling fruits and vegetables on a small scale

gymnosperm: Plants that contain two or more seeds leaves, and there is no special protective structure as seeds develop; instead, they develop on the outside bracts of cones.

gynoecious: plants that are all female

hand cleaning: removing plant debris by plant

hardening off: moving immature plants outdoors for a certain length of time each day, gradually increasing their exposure to the harsher outdoor conditions

heirloom plants: plant species handed down through generations

hermaphrodite: an organism that normally has both male and female sex organs

horticulturists: those who practice cultivating plants in a garden or nursery

hydrochory: seed dispersal made possible by water

hypocotl: a lower part of the embryonic stem

hypogeal: a plant that develops below ground

imperfect flowers: plants that have flowers that either contain pollen or eggs, but not both

king blossom: the largest and first flower to open

mechanical isolation: enclosing plants to prevent accidental cross-pollination

monocotyledon (monocot) seed: seeds with only one seed leaf

monoecious plants: plants with both male and female flowers

multicentric: plants that reproduce by enlarging and dividing underground

myrmecochory: seed dispersal using ants

nectaries: the nectar-secreting organ in a plant

outbreeding: another term for cross-pollination; pollination of two distinct parent plants

overwintering: when a plant spends the winter season in the ground

pegs: fertilized ovary spikes that grow down into the ground

perfect flowers: flowers that contain both ovules and pollen, the components necessary for plant reproduction

pistillate: female

plumule: the shoot that protrudes from the seed's embryo

pollination: the process where plant ovules must fertilize with pollen

radicle: a part of the seed embryo that develops as a seed root and eventually becomes the root system for the mature plant

roguing: systematically removing potential pollinators that might contribute negatively to the genetic makeup of the harvest

rooting hormone: a substance that stimulates plant cuttings to grow new roots when they come in contact with moist soil

rootstocks: trees that are grown specifically for their root portions to graft cuttings onto

scarification: altering a seed's coat to allow air and water into a seed, which initiates germination

seed coat: a protective layer around the inner parts of the seed that develops from the material tissue that initially surrounded the ovule

seed-set: how long it takes the plant to set seeds

seed-to-root-to-seed method: Using this method, a plant must be dug up, prepared, and stored at optimal conditions to survive the winter; this method is usually chosen in areas where there are harsh winters as opposed to allowing the plant to remain in the ground.

seed-to-seed method: Gardeners sow seed in the spring of the plant's first growing season. It is tended and prepared for the winter, and during the second year of growth, the plant reaches reproductive maturity and develops seeds for harvest at the end of the season.

seedlings: the first young plants that sprout

self-incompatible plants: All the flowers on a plant are sterile to each other.

selfing: a plant's ability to fertilize itself

staminate: male

stratification: artificially recreating the cold conditions a seed experiences during the winter prior to starting the germination process

taping: a form of mechanical isolation where gardeners use tape to close flowers that are about to bloom to prevent pollination from occurring

testa: the seed coat

thinning: removing a certain number of plants so sturdier, healthier specimens have a better chance of survival

threshing: breaking up plant material and exposing the seeds by stomping, beating, or crushing the seed-containing portions of the plant

trellis: any flat, one-dimensional structure that is made of metal, wood, or other material that can be used as a brace on which to train plants

umbels: the characteristic flowers of the Umbelliferae family

vernalization: exposure to cold temperatures over a few weeks

winnowing: separating the plant material from seed with a light wind

zoochory: seed dispersal where animals carry parent plants to the location where seed will germinate

Bibliography

Ashworth, Suzanne and Kent Whealy. *Seed to Seed: Seed Saving and Growing Techniques for Vegetables*. Decorah, Iowa: Seed Savers Exchange, 2002.

Bubel, Nancy. *The New Seed Starter's Handbook*. Emmaus, Pennsylvania: Rodale Books, 1988.

Deppe, Carol. *Breed Your Own Vegetable Varieties: The Gardener's & Farmer's Guide to Plant Breeding & Seed Saving*. White River Junction, Vermont: Chelsea Green, 2000.

Rogers, Marc and Polly Alexander. *Saving Seeds: The Gardener's Guide to Growing and Storing Vegetable and Flower Seeds (A Down-to-Earth Gardening Book)*. North Adams, Massachusetts: Storey Publishing, 1991.

Turner, Caroline B. *Seed Sowing and Saving: Step-by-Step Techniques for Collecting and Growing More than 100 Vegetables, Flowers, and Herbs*. North Adams, Massachusetts: Storey Publishing, 1998.

Author Biography

Born in Stuttgart, Germany, Katie spent most of her life moving from one place to the next, first as an Army brat, and then as a proud member of the United States Air Force. She is both an Air Force geospatial intelligence analyst and an Air Force historian. Through her many moves, Katie has learned a thing or two about gardening in a wide range of climates and seasons. She learned most of what she knows about plants and plant life from the family gardeners who surrounded her growing up but also picked up knowledge from a breadth of professionals and friends along the way.

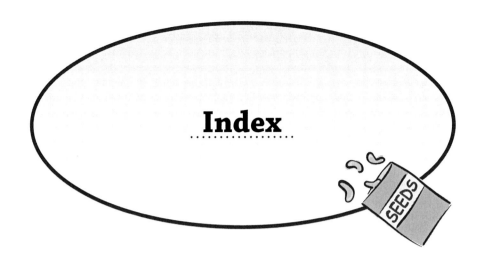

Index